ONLY IN
CANADA

ONLY IN
CANADA

The Wonders, Wilds, and Wisdom of the True North

CARRIE SHOOK
and
ROBERT L. SHOOK

A Perigee Book

Perigee Books
are published by
The Putnam Publishing Group
200 Madison Avenue
New York, NY 10016

Library of Congress Cataloging-in-Publication Data

Shook, Carrie
    Only in Canada : the wonders, wilds, and wisdom of the true
north / by Carrie Shook and Robert L. Shook.
        p.   cm.
    ISBN 0-399-51554-2
    1. Canada—Descripton and travel—1981—Guide-books.
    2. Canada—Civilization.   I. Shook, Robert L., date.
    II. Title.
F1009.S48   1990   89-38935 CIP
917.104'647—dc20

Printed in the United States of America
        1   2   3   4   5   6   7   8   9   10

ACKNOWLEDGMENTS

We would like to thank the following people for their tremendous contributions: Andre Bertrand, Buddy Brooks, Sharon Clark, Georges Humbert Couturier, Marla J. Daniels, Kathy Dobbin, John E. Dunn, Liz Fauteux, Gilles Gosselin, Nancy Harris, Sanford Horowitz, Anne Jones, Steve Johnston, Monique Juneau, Warren Lawrence, Mary Liff, Jeff Meyer, Howard F. Muchnick, Anne Johnson Myers, S. Namour, Jason Plummer, Don Robertson, Joseph Romain, Tim Ruddy, Jacob C. Sherman, Mike Shook, R. J. Shook, Becky Smith, Annie Bell Taylor, David Tornes, Giovanni Venturino, Wes Wenhardt, Monica Wolk, Mayor Brad Woodside, and Al Zuckerman.

We would also like to thank the chambers of commerce throughout Canada that gave us their valuable assistance; Barkerville Historic Town, Bexley Public Library, Café de la Paix Restaurant, Cariboo Tourist Association, Calgary Exhibition and Stampede, Canada's Capital Visitors and Convention Bureau, Casa Loma, Dionne Quints Museum, Edmonton Convention & Tourism Authority, Galérie le Chariot, Gambrinus Restaurant, Government of New Brunswick, Greater Montreal Convention and Tourism Bureau, Hockey Hall of Fame and Museum, Hôtel le Manoir d'Auteuil, Maid of the Mist Corporation, Metropolitan Toronto Convention & Visitors Association, Newfoundland Development and Tourism, Niagara Falls Museum, North Bay & District Chamber of Commerce, Quebec City Region

Tourism and Convention Bureau, Royal Canadian Mounted Police, British Columbia Ministry of Tourism and Provincial Secretary, Travel Manitoba, and West Edmonton Mall.

Special Acknowledgment

We would like to thank our editors, Lindley Boegehold and Tina Isaac, for their creative force and dedicated effort.

Contents

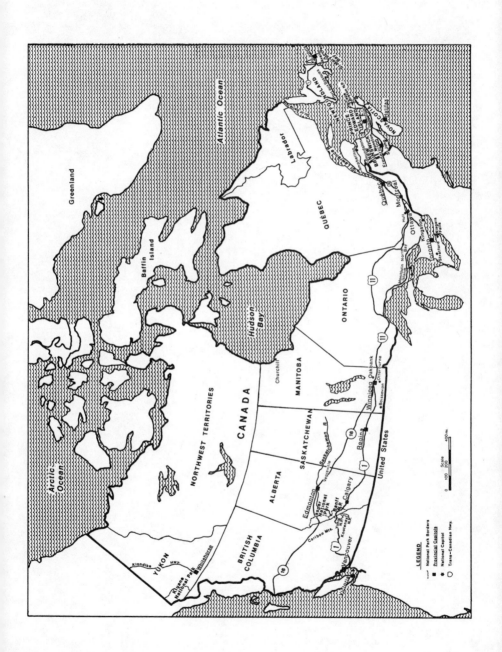

Introduction

Few places in the world can rival Canada's natural beauty. This nation is the world's second largest, bounded by more oceans than any other country in the world: Pacific, Atlantic, and Arctic (hence its motto, "From Sea to Sea"). 3.8 million square miles encompass some of the world's largest lakes and thousands of smaller ones, accounting for more than one-third of the world's fresh water. Its landscape ranges from rich rain forests to a rolling prairie, from rugged mountains to a craggy seacoast. The United States, Canada's only land neighbor, shares the longest unpatrolled border in the world. The Arctic region of Canada covers almost one million square miles, one-third of the country's land mass.

Explorer Jacques Cartier of the Breton port of Saint-Malo is credited for the name Canada. He first entered this unknown land by sailing the Gulf of St. Lawrence in 1534 in search of a passageway to the Orient. The following year, in what is now Quebec City, Cartier met a native Indian who spoke of "kanata," meaning a village or a group of huts, and Cartier mistook this word as the name of the country.

Shortly after Cartier's arrival, the French, British, and Portuguese began establishing colonies; however, they were not the first Europeans to settle in the New World. Around 1000 A.D., Norsemen found their way to regions that they named Helluland, Markland, and Vinland. Historians believe that current day Baffin Island was Helluland, Labrador was Markland, and Newfoundland was Vinland. As a nation, Canada only dates back to 1867, when its four provinces (Upper Canada, now Quebec, Lower Canada, now Ontario, New Brunswick, and Nova Scotia) were united by the British North America Act. The Canadian national flag, a red maple leaf against a white background bordered by two vertical red panels, only dates to 1964. The last traces of colonial status were finally eliminated with the passage of the Constitution Act of 1982.

Today's Canada is not only divided by region but also by a variety of ethnic origins, languages, and cultures. Canada's total population of 25 million is comprised of 45 percent British origin, 29 percent French, 25 percent other European, Asian, African, Inuit, and Ukrainian, among others. Official languages are both English and French. Montreal is the second largest French-speaking city in the world, but you will also hear Gaelic when visiting Nova Scotia and many other languages ranging from Italian to Viet-

The changing of the guard on Ottawa's Parliament Hill. (Courtesy Canada's Capitol Visitors and Convention Bureau)

namese throughout the country. Canada is a sparsely settled country—an overwhelming majority of people (around 90%) live within two hundred miles of the United States border.

The pristine beauty and abundance of natural resources which first attracted early colonists continue to attract millions of tourists from around the world.

The Hudson Bay Company

At one time, the majority of Canada was owned by the Hudson Bay Company, chartered in 1670 by Charles II of Great Britain. Headed by Prince Rupert, the Hudson Bay Company (commonly known as the H.B.C.) possessed more property than any other private enterprise. The H.B.C.'s holdings covered over one-twelfth of the earth's surface and its domain stretched thousands of miles, from London across Canada, through California and across the Pacific to Hawaii—over three million square miles (ten times the size of the Holy Roman Empire at its peak). The H.B.C.'s influence, however, stretched even beyond these limits, and it became the largest private enterprise in the world, eventually giving birth to the country of Canada.

The Hudson Bay Company imported, exported, and traded an immense variety of goods from around the world. Its most valuable commodity was fur, for which Canada became a mecca, with beaver the most prized of all furs trapped in Canada. This is one of the few animals to profoundly influence the making of a country. From the early 1650s to the late 1850s, men crossed oceans, lived, and died for beaver skin. Beaver was more valuable than gold, and there was a huge demand for it throughout Europe.

The popularity of beaver fur dates back to biblical times when it was worn by King Solomon. At the peak of the H.B.C.'s success, beaver hats were one of the ultimate status symbols. Beaver headpieces were so valuable they were willed from father to son.

Warehouses where beaver fur was stored were swept clean daily, and the dust was carefully sifted for stray beaver hairs. For more than 150 years in Canada, beaver pelts were used as currency. At an H.B.C. trading post, trappers used beaver pelts to purchase everything from sugar, gunpowder, and thread to blankets, brandy, and tobacco.

For many years, the Hudson Bay Company controlled one-third of the untouched northern part of the American continent. The company's pursuit of precious beaver fur was responsible for the vast exploration and white settlements established here. The first fort in the area was Fort St. Pierre, built in 1731, on the south side of Pither's Point, the oldest continually occupied white settlement west of the Great Lakes.

The Hudson Bay Company, once the most prominent name in Canada, still remains an important part of the nation's history, considered by many to have been "a kingdom of its own." Its enormous impact on the formation of Canada was geographical, social, and political as the history of nearly all regions began with fur trade under the H.B.C.'s control. The H.B.C. kept ambitious American settlers and the U.S. border from moving north, earning the nickname, "Here Before Christ." In 1870, the H.B.C. sold its territory to Canada, and its forts Garry (later Winnipeg), Edmonton, and Victoria became provincial capitals.

The Hudson Bay Company is still the oldest capitalist corporation in the world. It has survived and prospered through 300 years of change: war, rebellion, bureaucracy, and the birth of a nation, and remains a major force in Canadian commerce.

The Royal Canadian Mounted Police

"Maintain the Right" is the official motto of the Royal Canadian Mounted Police (R.C.M.P.), a motto still enforced throughout Canada. In today's Canada the mounties' black horses and traditional scarlet tunics are only seen during ceremonial occasions.

R.C.M.P. history began when the huge territory stretching west from the Red River for 1,000 miles to the Rockies was known as Rupert's Land (1670–1870). King Charles II had granted the largely uninhabited land to the Hudson Bay Company, which then sold the territory to the Dominion of Canada in 1870. Several settlements were organized, including the Province of Manitoba (roughly the size of Texas). The North-West Mounted Police came into existence in 1873, a police force of 300 organized by Governor-General Lord Dufferin. Their immediate objectives were to stop liquor traffic among the Indians, to gain their respect and confidence, halt tribal warfare and attacks on white settlers, and collect customs dues.

The North-West Mounted Police was the sole police force in Canada's Arctic. The force maintained law and order during the Klondike Gold Rush and played an important role in opening up Canada's Arctic frontier. In 1920, the Mounted Police was renamed the Royal Canadian Mounted Police.

Today, the R.C.M.P. is one of the most dynamic and ad-

The R.C.M.P. in "Bridal Arch" and "Dome" formations.
(Courtesy the R.C.M.P.)

vanced crime-fighting organizations in the world. Head-quartered in Ottawa, the R.C.M.P. has exclusive police jurisdiction in the Yukon and Northwest Territories, and offers protection to over 150 municipalities across Canada.

A grand, colorful parade by foremost police officers, the traditional R.C.M.P. Musical Ride tours throughout Canada and the world, entertaining millions of spectators year-round. After serving two or three years of active police work, officers can volunteer for a two-year long duty with the Musical Ride. After an intensive training course and a grueling selection process, thirty-two candidates are chosen to be Canadian ambassadors of goodwill. The R.C.M.P. horses undergo an intense two-and-a-half year training program to prepare them for elaborate ceremonies, so they are able to stand at attention unbothered by loud brass bands and large enthusiastic crowds.

During summertime, mounted escorts accompany the state carriage on Ottawa's Sussex Drive. Royal processions over the years include Queen Victoria's Diamond Jubilee (1897), the coronations of King Edward VII (1902), King George V (1911), King George VI (1937), and Queen Elizabeth II (1953). A mounted contingent was also present at the Silver Jubilee procession of Queen Elizabeth II in London in 1977.

Because the rider and his horse must be in sync, the Musical Ride demands utmost control, timing, and coordination. The riders perform a series of intricate formations including the "Bridal Arch," the "X," the "Shanghai Cross," the "Maze," and the "Dome." The highlight of each performance is the "Charge," when the riders lower their lances and ride their horses forward in a line at a full gallop. The performance concludes with the "March Past," with riders saluting the guest of honor.

For information regarding performance location, dates, and time of the Musical Rides performances, please call their information hotline at (613) 993–3751.

The Stratford Shakespeare Festival

Canada's premier theater attraction takes place in Stratford, a small community in Ontario with a population of just over 26,000. Home to the internationally known annual Stratford Shakespeare Festival, the small town is reminiscent of the original Stratford-Upon-Avon in Great Britain, where William Shakespeare was born, and where his plays have been performed for centuries.

The festival started over twenty-five years ago and has become a world theatrical event with performances in three theaters. Not only are the works of Shakespeare featured, but the plays of other prominent dramatists, such as Molière, Jonson, Chekhov, and Ibsen, are presented as well. Also performed throughout the season, which lasts from May through October, are contemporary drama and musicals. In addition, you can attend a number of lectures offered by world-renowned authorities who speak on topics ranging from Elizabethan drama to Shakespeare's personal life.

The festival accommodates audiences numbering over 2,200 daily. International stars perform on a modern-day version of an Elizabethan stage that has seven acting levels, nine major entrances, a balcony, and several trapdoors.

The Stratford Shakespeare Festival is a great theater experience in a comfortable outdoor setting. For more information call (519) 271–4040 or (519) 273–1600 for tickets.

A Living National Treasure:
The Canadian Quints

These five little girls affected the lives of millions even before their first birthday. A unique Canadian national treasure is a set of quintuplets whose birth was announced around the globe. The Dionne Quints, born on May 28, 1934 in North Bay, Ontario are the first quintuplets known to survive to adulthood. In order of their birth, the Quints were named Yvonne, Annette, Cecile, Emilie, and Marie. Magazines and newspapers around the world have followed the Quints throughout their lives.

The Quints' combined birth-weight was thirteen pounds, six ounces. Their parents already had five other children, and their expected sixth pushed the total to ten kids. Assuming guardianship of the five girls, the Ontarian government built a mansion across the road from the Dionne family farm. As infants, they were raised in isolation with occasional visits by family members under controlled conditions and supervision. Statistics gave the Dionne sisters only a 75 percent chance of reaching maturity together.

The Quints inspired movies, sponsored a number of products, and were an important contribution to the tourist industry. During the Depression, the public craved an honest-to-goodness, human-interest success story, and the Quints' survival fit the bill perfectly. Thousands of people followed the Quints every step, much as they do the whereabouts of the British royal family.

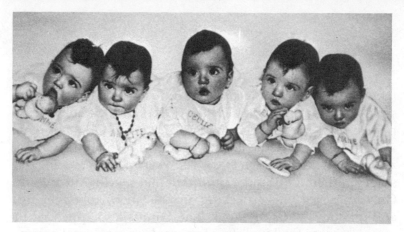

The Dionne Quints at several months and five years of age.
(Courtesy Dionne Quints Museum)

In 1937 the Quints were first put on public view at their home four times a day, attracting as many as 6,000 admirers per showing. During the first two years, it is estimated that the Quints drew $20 million each year in revenue for the province. Over the years, hundreds of thousands of fans stood outside the mansion's gates to watch the five little girls play in their private yard.

21

Today, hundreds of collectors search for Quint-inspired memorabilia. Such collectibles include the Brown & Bigelow series of Quint calendars (1936–1955) and Palmolive teaspoons, each bearing the name of a Quint. Other sought-after items include the advertisements in which the Quints appear as children, such as the Karo syrup ads featuring the sisters gathered around a pumpkin and playing during the Christmas season—frolicking in the snow, tobogganing, and mailing letters to Santa. The Quints also appeared in endorsements for Lysol disinfectant, Colgate dental cream, and Quaker oats, among others.

In addition, sets of commemorative dolls were sold around the world. The Quint dolls manufactured by the Alexander Doll Company in New York City from 1935–1939 are the most famous, but dolls modeled after the girls were produced by nearly every doll company in North America. The dolls are now worth hundreds of dollars.

Three films were produced starring the five Dionne sisters. They costarred with Jean Hersholt in *The Country Doctor, Reunion,* and *Five of a Kind.* The world premier of *The Country Doctor* took place in New York and Toronto in 1936.

On May 22, 1939, His Majesty King George VI and the queen met the Quints in the Parliament Buildings in Toronto, the first time the girls had ever been away from their nursery. Elaborate preparations were made: the Quints were transported to Toronto in a special train and then were escorted by a team of highly trained policemen and other government officials. The Quints once again met with British royalty in 1951, when Princess Elizabeth (now Queen Elizabeth II) visited North Bay.

When the girls were old enough to go to school, the classroom came to them. Around their sixth birthday, the nursery was renovated and converted into a special school. Ten French-Canadian girls of approximately the same age were selected to attend the school in order to provide the Quints with a normal school atmosphere. Five chosen students were English-speaking in order to help the Quints with their English.

Annette was the first of the Quints to marry when she became the wife of a Montreal financier, Germain Allard, in 1957. Later that year, Cecile married Philippe Langlois, a technician for Canadian Broadcasting Corporation (CBC), and she was the first to become a mother. In 1958, Marie was married to Florian Houle. None of the Quints had multiple births. At the age of 20, Emilie was the first Quint to die following a stroke in 1954. Marie died at the age of 36 in 1970.

The government-built Dionne mansion remained vacant for twenty years after the Quints' departure. Currently, it is a nursing home, renamed Nipissing Manor.

Today, the North Bay and district chamber of commerce is offering 33mm-nickel trade dollars to commemorate the fiftieth anniversary of the birth of the Quints. Legal tender in 1984, these coins are now valuable collector's items. The Dionne family home is a museum displaying hundreds of photographs of the Quints throughout their lives. A large collection of the girls' personal belongings are on display, including the gowns they wore when they were introduced to King George VI and Queen Elizabeth, their original bassinet, and five eyedroppers used to feed the tiny infants. The museum is open from mid-May to mid-October from 9 A.M. to 5 P.M., except during July and August, when the hours are 9 A.M. to 9 P.M. daily. Although the museum is closed during the winter, the gift shop and a small exhibition remain open. The museum is located on 1375 Seymour Street in North Bay at the intersection of Highways 17 and 11. For more information call (705) 472–8480.

Canadian Museum of Civilization

A sojourn to this museum is like a visit to every province of Canada, a step back in history and into the future, all in one. The museum is approximately 100,000 square meters and has over 3.5 million artifacts, and state-of-the-art exhibitions in life-size settings displaying Canadian heritage with special effects and costumed guides. Don't plan on seeing everything. Allowing only three seconds per artifact, you'd need a full year of eight-hour days to see everything, so you'd better pick and choose!

On permanent exhibition are six houses built in the architectural styles developed by native American Indian tribes of the Pacific Coast. Represented are the six tribes of Coast Salish, Nuchaahnulth, Kwakiutl, Nuxalk, Haida, and Tsimshian, all from western Canada. These houses were built by members of Pacific Coast tribes and are exhibited at a boardwalk along a shoreline, highlighted by a backdrop with a forest scene that is the largest color photograph in the world. Also featured is a world-renowned collection of authentic totem poles. Native ceremonies and performances will provide you with a variety of cultural backgrounds and historical themes.

Under a high-dome is History Hall which displays one thousand years of Canadian history in a geographic and chronological "streetscape" in an exhibition space the size of a football field. Here, thirty-three settings describe Canada from east to west with hundreds of artifacts and activities that animate the story of the people who built the country. You will enter a variety of life-size homes, boats, churches, factories, and many other structures of the past representing each province.

Early European settling scenes include the recreation of a Norse landing in Newfoundland around 1000 A.D.; the interior of a Basque ship circa 1585, and a reconstructed whaling station from the subsequent period of New France (1600–1760) are on display, highlighted by settings of Acadian life, a Louisbourg tavern, a Quebec public square, a convent-hospital, an artisan's house in a farm setting, a town square in New France, and a turn-of-the-century railroad station.

The wilderness display for the period 1680–1860 reconstructs a fur-trading post, a covered "Conestoga" wagon, a logging enterprise, and a Metis settlement. It also features the opening of western Canada from 1870–1914 which is represented by a turn-of-the-century railway station leading to a small prairie town setting. Life in an industrial setting, 1890–1940, is depicted by a theme area which includes a Ukrainian church, a Winnipeg street scene, a clothing factory, and another theme area describing the nostalgia of childhood in Canada.

The final section of the modern Canada display chronicling 1940 to the present will take you through a cannery, a British Columbia logging scene, an exhibition on Yukon mining, and a scene illustrating the effect of modern development on traditional Northern life.

Perhaps the biggest attraction at the new museum is the only combined Imax and Omnimax film theater in the world—the theater of the future. The Imax is a large vertical screen covering the front wall of the cinema, ten times the size of a regular screen. It is twenty-six meters (eighty-seven feet) wide and nineteen meters (sixty-two feet) high and quickly slides out of sight when the huge Omnimax

25

screen is in operation. The Omnimax screen is domed above the audience, twenty-three meters (seventy-six feet) in diameter. Subjects like space travel and underwater exploration are shown so convincingly, you'll believe you are actually there. The theater holds 295 people in an intimate, steep auditorium with tilting seats which allow you a comfortable and comprehensive view of the surrounding screens. Films are shown on a daily basis.

The museum is located at 100 Laurier Street in Hull, Quebec and directly faces the Parliament Hill of Ottawa. The view of the Parliament from the museum is the same as shown on the back of the Canadian $1.00 bill. During the summer months, the museum is open daily from 10 A.M. to 5 P.M. During the winter, hours of operation are 10 A.M. to 5 P.M. daily and on Thursdays 10 A.M. to 8 P.M. The museum is closed on Mondays and Christmas Day and offers free admission on Thursdays year-round. Call (613) 992–3497 for a recorded message.

Art of the Canadian Arctic

The Inuits, the Native American Indians of Arctic Canada, for years referred to as Eskimos, are the creators of an art that is unequaled anywhere else in the world. For centuries, the Inuits have depended on their ability to create with their hands the necessities of everyday existence, such as carved objects for decoration, rituals, entertainment, and, later, for trade.

Over the past thirty years, people in the outside world have taken a great interest in Inuit art and culture. Each carver develops an individual style for subject matter, type of material, and methods used. One carver may choose to carve mostly animals, yet another may choose to carve Inuits in everyday life. Stone is the most frequently used material, though antler, bone, and ivory are also common. When whalebone is used, it is first tested to insure that it is over 200 years old.

Inuit sculptures are appreciated around the world as unique and valuable artwork. Because of their great popularity, there is a proliferation of mass-produced imitations, but the genuine carvings are protected by the Canadian government, which registers the symbol of the igloo as the trademark on each piece. Carvings bearing this igloo symbol are certified to be genuine handmade Inuit pieces.

A unique Canadian art form, the sculptures allow the Inuits to share their culture with the rest of the world. The art has become the primary source of capital for Arctic communities: prices range from hundreds of dollars for small pieces to tens of thousands for larger pieces. Buying Inuit art can be a valuable investment but Americans should be aware that it is illegal to bring whalebone into the United States. All other materials are acceptable.

A great place to shop or just browse is at the Galérie Le Chariot in Old Montreal. Looking more like a museum than a retail store, the art gallery specializes in Inuit art and displays an extensive collection. Open daily from 10 A.M. to 6 P.M., it is located at 446 Place Jacques Cartier. Le Chariot ships Inuit art all over the world. Call (514) 875–4994 or (514) 875–6134 for more information.

West Edmonton Mall:
The Eighth Wonder of the World

Where would you expect to find 800 stores, 110 restaurants, nineteen movie theaters, a replica of the Santa Maria, an N.H.L.-size hockey rink, the world's largest indoor water-park, the world's largest indoor amusement park, submarine rides, and an eighteen-hole miniature golf course all under one roof? Welcome to the world's largest shopping arena, the West Edmonton Mall.

The Guinness Book of World Records lists the Edmonton, Alberta mall, equivalent in size to forty-eight city blocks, as larger than any other mall in the world—and by a long shot. The $1.1 billion mall contains 5.2 million square feet of entertainment and has parking to accommodate more than 20,000 cars. Edmonton has a population of approximately 569,000, and over 15,000 locals are employed by the mall. Visitors travel to see the mall from all over the globe.

The World Waterpark has sensational slides, a wild surf, and six-foot waves. The sun shines year-round above a huge swimming pool. Having a party? The pool will accommodate up to 5,000 of your closest friends! There are seventeen giant water slides starting at heights of eighty-five feet. Swimming, surfing, suntanning, and kayaking in a tropical atmosphere makes a great day at the West Edmonton Mall beach any day of the year.

Deep-Sea Adventure transports visitors to an underwater kingdom beneath the mall. Four authentic submarines

The indoor swimming pool at West Edmonton Mall. (Courtesy West Edmonton Mall)

(more than are owned by the Canadian Navy) complete with underwater cameras and sonar equipment plunge beneath the depths of the Great Barrier Reef, which contains exotic fish, bottlenose dolphins, sharks, barracudas, sunken treasure, and a hand-carved replica of Christopher Columbus' Santa Maria. There are also courses available in scuba diving and underwater photography.

The world's largest indoor amusement park is bound to entertain young and old alike. Its 400,000 square-foot park offers dozens of rides and attractions, including "The Mindbender," the world's largest triple-loop roller coaster. There are bumper cars, a Ferris wheel, a hand-carved carousel, a petting zoo, and a huge electric train.

For wildlife and nature enthusiasts, there are twenty-five saltwater aquariums containing over 500 species of sea life. Ten bird aviaries exhibit birds from South and West Africa, China, and India. The safari-like African environment is home to Siberian tigers, black bears, and chimpanzees. Tropical jungles with parrots, toucans, and flamingos are surrounded by statues in a luxurious setting of brass, glass, and marble.

This incredible shopping mall provides a fascinating combination of fashion, fun, and fantasy. Over 100 restaurants represent gourmet cuisine from around the world. Bourbon Street, a replica of the original in New Orleans, offers thirteen bars and restaurants for evening entertainment with an atmosphere of an open-air, starry night. Europa Boulevard is modeled after a typical European street, featuring internationally known fashion boutiques.

An exclusive art collection containing some of the rarest pieces in the world features priceless vases from the Ching Dynasty and a valuable solid ivory, hand-carved pagoda from the Ming Dynasty. Replicas of the Crown Jewels of the British Empire from William I to George VI are on display, as well as swords, sceptres, crowns, and maces.

The Fantasyland Hotel of the West Edmonton Mall is where dreams come true in a fantasy-like atmosphere. The hotel offers period rooms in colorful themes. The Roman Room, for example, is a reminder of the period of Anthony and Cleopatra, complete with white marble statues, a round velvet-covered bed with silk draperies, and a genuine Roman bath. The Hollywood Room has neon lighting, a patented carpet covered with twinkling lights, and a black-tile spa surrounded by neon stars. Guests who stay in the Polynesian Room will sleep on a water bed in a warrior catamaran equipped with a full sail, and relax in a hot tub modeled after an erupting volcano. There is also a waterfall emptying into a rock pool. You'll find six other hotels in the vicinity, but none that offer the wonders of Fantasyland Hotel! For reservations, call (800) 661–6454 (in Canada) or (403) 444–3000.

The West Edmonton Mall, the city under one roof, is

packed with entertainment and activities for all ages. Shopping hours are from 10 A.M. to 9 P.M. Monday through Friday, 10 A.M. to 6 P.M. Saturday, and 12 P.M. to 6 P.M. on Sunday. Attractions, theaters, and restaurants are open late for your enjoyment. For more information, call (800) 661–8890.

Casa Loma

A castle in Toronto suitable for a king made a pauper out of the man who hoped to call it home. Canada's Casa Loma is a magnificent ninety-eight-room medieval-style castle smack in the heart of Toronto. It was the first castle in the world with an indoor swimming pool and an electric elevator within its stately towers. Complete with soaring battlements, secret passageways, and sweeping terraces, it rests on a hill, high above the city. The landmark was built between 1911 and 1914 by a famous Canadian, Sir Henry Pellatt, a soldier, financier, and industrialist.

Born in 1859 in Kingston, Ontario, Sir Henry Mill Pellatt was the eldest of six children. He graduated from the Upper Canada College and became an avid traveler. During his travels, he became fascinated by art, antiques, military tradition, and especially castles, which he measured, memorized, and sketched. In his late teens, he joined his father's stockbroking business and the Queen's Own Rifles, a volunteer battalion of which he became commanding officer. A tremendous athlete, Pellatt won the North American Champion Race at the age of twenty, finishing the last 100 yards in twelve seconds, an accomplishment not equaled until 1930 by champion Jesse Owens.

Pellatt laid the foundation of his fortune by a shrewd investment in stock of the Northwest Land Company. He purchased stock at $12 and $14 a share, and when the stock quadrupled in price, Pellatt came out with a profit over $3 million. His next investment, in the stock of Canadian Pacific Railway, was again successful.

At twenty, Pellatt organized the Toronto Electric Light Company, the first in the city. Later, he organized the Electrical Development Company and the Niagara Power Company. During his successful business career, he served on the board of directors for many of the top corporations in North America. Throughout his life, Sir Henry continued his strong interest in the military. He expanded the Queen's Own Rifles into a regiment and was appointed brigadier-general in 1916. In 1921, he was raised to the rank of major-general.

Pellatt was an incurable romantic who had a lifelong interest in medieval castles of Europe. After building his huge fortune, he decided to build a castle he could call his own.

Second only to the Vanderbilt's Biltmore House in North Carolina, Casa Loma is the largest home on this continent. After spending several years studying old-world castles and gathering materials and furnishings, Pellatt began to build the grand estate in 1911. He hired Edward Lennox, a famous Canadian architect, who combined all of Sir Henry's favorite castle sketches into one colossal medieval structure. Sir Henry personally interviewed each of the 300 workmen and brought Scottish stonemasons from Europe to Canada to build the massive stone wall surrounding the six-acre site. He bought marble, glass, and paneling in Europe, teak in Asia, and oak and walnut from prime areas of North America. It was his final intention to leave the castle to the city to be used as a historical and military museum. Although Sir Henry planned to spend $250,000 on the entire house, the costs surpassed his estimate and he spent that much on the wall alone.

Over three years, it took more than 300 workmen to build Casa Loma, and costs totaled over 3.5 million dollars. Upon its completion, many believed it was the most romantic thing to ever happen to Toronto. Others agreed with a local critic who called it a masterful mix of seventeenth-century Scotland and Twentieth-Century Fox.

One of the greatest features of the castle is the Great Hall, which has a lofty seventy-foot oak-beamed ceiling, a forty-foot-high window and an Italian marble floor. Bronze-and-glass doors lead into a conservatory which has a stained-glass dome backlit by 600 lights. Here, steampipes buried in the flowerbeds provided heating for Sir Henry's tropical plants. The dining room is large enough to comfortably seat over 100 guests. Although Sir Henry rarely read, his library had room for over 10,000 volumes. The study where he worked on business matters had several concealed passages that allowed him to elude guests or, eventually, creditors. One secret stairway led up to the second floor, and another down to the wine cellar. There are hundreds of other fascinating features throughout the house, including hand-carved gargoyles from Europe brought home by Sir Henry. The 800-foot tunnel, eighteen feet beneath the road, connects the castle to the horse stables, hunting lodge, exercise room, greenhouses, boilers, and the mushroom-growing rooms.

The castle has its own telephone system, a $75,000 pipe organ, marble swimming pool, and a huge kitchen range capable of roasting an entire ox. There are fifteen baths and 5,000 electric lights. The wine cellar was considered to be the greatest on the continent.

The expense of maintaining the castle was enormous. It required more than forty servants, property taxes were $12,000 annually and the heating bill was always over $25,000 a year. Unfortunately, after the many years of construction, the Pellatts were only able to stay at the castle from 1914 to 1923. When World War I began, construction on the castle was forced to stop prematurely. Sir Henry continued to host several grand events, usually held outside, as the interior of the castle was mostly unfinished. In 1923 the Home Bank went bankrupt, leaving Sir Henry's company more than $1.7 million in the red. Shortly thereafter, Lady Pellatt died of a heart attack, and Sir Henry was forced to move out of Casa Loma. In a five-day long auction following his departure, the $1.5 million in furnishings netted only $250,000. "It is a sale which breaks my heart," Pellatt said to a reporter. A bison head in bronze, which had cost Sir Henry $1,000, sold for only $50, less than the worth of the metal alone. Thousands of books sold at a flat price of 60 cents each, and Oriental rugs sold at a fraction of their worth.

Sir Henry, who had once been worth over $17 million, died a poor man at the age of eighty in the home belonging to his chauffeur. His funeral was the largest in Toronto's history.

After the castle closed down, the city considered using it for many things including a home for war veterans, a high

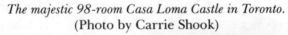

The majestic 98-room Casa Loma Castle in Toronto.
(Photo by Carrie Shook)

The conservatory at Casa Loma. (Photo by Carrie Shook)

school, convent, and a lodge. Toronto's leading lady, Mary Pickford, tried to use it in her movies. Eventually, Casa Loma was opened as an exclusive apartment hotel, but it soon failed. After many years of neglect, the castle was leased in 1936 by the city of Toronto to the Kiwanis Club which has been operating Casa Loma as a public museum ever since.

Six acres of magnificent gardens featuring sculptures and a woodland preserve with a water course have been restored by the Garden Club of Toronto. The house is filled with nineteenth-century antiques, though few actually belonged to Sir Henry.

Casa Loma is open daily from 10 A.M. to 4 P.M. except Christmas Day and New Year's Day. It is located at 1 Austin Terrace in Toronto. Call (416) 923–1171 for more information.

Le Jardin Botanique:
Montreal Botanical Garden

The world's most beautiful flowers and plants bloom year-round at the largest botanical garden in North America located in Montreal. Le Jardin Botanique features over thirty outdoor gardens, ten greenhouses, and approximately 26,000 species and varieties of flora. As many as two million people a year visit the garden that plays an important role as a scientific and educational institution. The seventy-three-hectare (180 acres) garden was founded in 1931 by botanist frère Marie-Victorin (1885–1944) and is owned by the city of Montreal. Well known for the quality and diversity of its collection, the garden faces the site of the 1976 Summer Olympic Games.

Thirty outdoor gardens feature just about every type of design imaginable including marsh, annuals, perennials, rose, and Japanese gardens. The Perennial Garden consists of vast symmetrical flower beds, planted with different varieties of tulips, daffodils, and crocuses during spring, then African marigolds and Zanzibar balsams in summer and fall. In the Monastery Garden, medicinal and aromatic plants are grown and arranged to mimic the medicinal herb gardens kept in the Middle Ages. Plants used in the monastic orders around 812 A.D. during the time of Charlemagne are found here, including the European wildginger, common chicory, spearmint, and parsnip. The Medicinal Plant

Garden offers over 100 specimens used in both folk medicine and today's pharmaceutical industry, such as yellow gentian and common foxglove. The Rose Garden has a collection of over 8,000 rose bushes that are displayed in 100 flower beds. Roses bloom from mid-June to the end of summer.

The twenty-five-hectares Japanese Garden is known around the world and is especially wonderful to visit in spring when the cherry trees and magnolias are in full bloom. Every tree, shrub, and stone in the Japanese Garden has been carefully chosen and placed, and each has a symbolic significance. The pond's series of cascades and springs express life and renewal. Modeled after traditional Japanese gardens, this Japanese oasis is designed for meditation and peace. The Japanese Garden Pavilion serves as a cultural center (for the Montreal Japanese community) and has an exhibition hall, tearoom, and library focusing on Japanese history. World-known landscape architect Ken Nakajima, assisted by a botanical garden staff and a Quebec-based landscaping design firm, conceived and meticulously designed this garden with financial assistance from the governments of Japan, Quebec, Canada, Montreal, and various Japanese firms. This is a place where you can escape the rapid pace of the city and where harmony is a way of life.

The new exhibition greenhouse is the largest of its kind in the country, providing an enchanting background for the seasonal exhibitions and collections. There are carnivorous plants, giant water lilies from Amazonia measuring more than two meters in diameter and other tropical plants from every corner of the globe. The greenhouse also exhibits the largest collection of bonsai and Penjing outside Asia. This is the worlds' only collection that includes specimens from three recognized schools of this art: the schools of Japan, China, and Hong Kong.

You mustn't visit Montreal without stopping to enjoy its

world-famous botanical garden. The outdoor gardens are open daily from sunrise to sunset and are free of charge. The greenhouses are open daily from 9 A.M. to 6 P.M. It is located at 4101 Sherbrooke Street East. Call (514) 872–1400 for more information.

First City of the Twenty-first Century

When the combination of wind and freezing rain make you miserable and you want to spend the day in a warm climate browsing in boutiques, there is still hope if you are in Montreal!

Montreal, a booming international metropolis where temperatures soar and plummet from season to season, has found an answer to the bad weather blues: a weatherproof, underground city for pedestrians only. It is an innovation that has made Montreal a pleasant place to visit or live in any weather, and is the prototype of the future.

Throughout the year, you can stroll through the underground city in a comfortable 72 degree F. temperature. The broad, colorful concourses are lined with boutiques, restaurants, department stores, and just about anything else you would expect to find in a large downtown area. The high-ceilinged passageways are filled with plants and trees, and are an airy escape from the world upstairs.

The underground city began in the early 1960s, when several downtown buildings and the metro system were being constructed. Underground passageways were built connecting downtown buildings and, by 1988, over fifteen kilometers of underground passages were open, giving pedestrians access to virtually every type of facility without ever venturing outside.

Now over 4-million square meters in size, the underground city connects two railway stations, a bus terminal,
2000 commercial addresses, six major hotels, 3000 housing
units, and the University of Quebec at Montreal. Inside are
three large department stores, 1400 boutiques, 200 restaurants, thirty bank branches, thirty cinemas and theaters,
and two exhibition halls.

There are a number of entryways to the underground city.
In the downtown area, you simply take an escalator down
from one of the commercial complexes. The underground
city is constantly growing; each new building constructed
downtown is linked to the underground city through a passageway.

Another underground city has been built in Toronto.
Toronto locals claim theirs is the world's largest subterra-
nean complex, with Montreal's being the second. Deep beneath the streets, the Toronto underground stretches six
blocks and encompasses more than 1000 stores, restaurants,
banks, and offices. There are three miles of tunnels and
seven subway stops, enough for a day-long adventure! The
famous Eaton Centre, a shopping mall designed to resemble
a ship, is connected to the underground. The ambiance of
the underground also includes living trees and plants, some
as tall as twenty feet. Canada's underground cities just might
be the wave of the future!

Tour the Universe in Toronto

The C.N. Tower in Toronto is the tallest freestanding structure in the world. Twice as tall as the Eiffel Tower in Paris, it is over 553.3 meters from the pool at its base to the tip of the transmission mast at the top and offers the best view of the city. The tower opened in 1976 and serves as a communications tower and a sight-seeing platform featuring a revolving restaurant and nightclub.

A glass-fronted elevator takes you up to the observation deck at the 346-meter level. On a clear day, you can see as far as Rochester, N.Y. and to the far shore of Lake Simcoe to the north. Located at 301 Front Street West, it is next to the famous SkyDome. The C.N. Tower, now the city's symbol, makes Toronto's skyline recognizable to the world. For information about tours, call (416) 360–8500.

Inside the C.N. Tower, you can tour the universe, complete with a trip to Jupiter! The C.N. Tower is tall, but it doesn't exactly reach as high as the atmosphere. The Tour of the Universe, set in the year 2019, celebrates the fiftieth anniversary of man's first steps on the moon in 1969. The tour begins in a fully functional airport leading to a wonderful simulated space flight complete with blast-off to Jupiter.

The sixty-minute long tour, developed with the assistance

of NASA, the National Research Center of Canada, and the National Museum of Science and Technology in Ottawa, is open year-round with expanded hours during summer from 10 A.M. to 10 P.M. Call (416) 363–TOUR for more information.

The SkyDome

The first stadium complex in the world with a fully retractable roof is now the pride of Toronto. The SkyDome provides world-class entertainment as the home to baseball's Toronto Blue Jays and Toronto Argonauts (Canadian Football League) as well as top musical performers in between games. This is no ordinary stadium: it has seating-capacity for 60,000, an 800-seat restaurant, a nightclub, a health club complete with swimming pool and track, and a 350-room hotel with seventy rooms overlooking the field.

The construction of the SkyDome was a formidable task which required 210,000 tons of concrete (enough to build a sidewalk from Toronto to Montreal (about 590 kilometers) and created 12,000 jobs. The retractable roof weighs over 9,000 tons and opens and closes within minutes. At its summit, the SkyDome is high enough to enclose a thirty-one-story apartment building. It also has the world's largest video display, a $6 million "SkyVision" that measures 33 feet high by 115 feet wide. The amount of light required to keep the stadium bright is enough to light a city of 25,000. The SkyDome will contribute about $326 million in annual income to metro Toronto.

You will never again have to worry about a sporting event being canceled due to bad weather. Expect to see clones of the SkyDome popping up around the world in the near future.

The World's Largest Easter Egg

In Vegreville, Alberta, the internationally known 5,000-pound (inedible) Pysanka egg is 25.7 feet long, 18 feet wide, and stands three stories high! And, in case you're wondering, a Pysanka is a Ukrainian Easter egg.

The Pysanka egg—the largest Easter egg in the world. (Courtesy Vegreville and District Chamber of Commerce)

The Pysanka structure in Vegreville links the present with the heritage and culture of the Ukrainians. The people of Vegreville chose to build a monument to represent the Ukrainians, Alberta's largest ethnic community. It is also a tribute to the one-hundredth anniversary of the Royal Canadian Mounted Police who provided security to the large multicultural settlement.

The giant egg, which reacts like a weather vane to the changes in the wind, is an achievement of mathematical, architectural, and engineering firsts. Professor Ronald Resch, a computer scientist at the University of Utah, developed the highly complex project with a complex, geometric computerized design. Resch's computer programs pieced together an immense jigsaw puzzle containing 524 star patterns, 1,108 equilateral triangles, 3,512 visible facets, 6,978 nuts and bolts, and 177 internal braces.

The design incorporates five distinct symbols. Radiating gold stars on the end sections symbolize life and good fortune. The series of three pointed stars in alternating gold and silver represent the Trinity, and the band of silver circumscribing the egg represents eternity. On the central barrel section are windmills of six vanes and points in gold and silver, symbolizing the protection and security provided by the Royal Canadian Mounted Police. The egg is decorated in gold, silver, and bronze, colors that represent prosperity.

The Canadian Sea Monster

Interested in turning a profit out of an adventurous vacation? If the answer is yes, visit Okanagan Lake in British Columbia where, upon capturing legendary sea monster Ogopogo, you could receive a hefty reward!

Reported to be a cousin to Scotland's world-known Loch Ness Monster, "Nessie," Ogopogo allegedly swims up and down the ninety-mile-long lake that stretches from Vernon to Kelowna and to Penticton at the south end of the lake. Sightings of Ogopogo have been reported over the years, and photographs have been taken supporting rumors of his existence. The famous sea monster has also been spotted at Kalamalka Lake, Vernon's "Lake of Many Colors," leading many to believe that Ogopogo uses underwater caves that run between the two lakes.

Rewards are offered to any party responsible for the live capture of Ogopogo. This provides incentive to the hundreds of sea vessels full of curious tourists and experienced sea hunters who visit each year to search for the mysterious sea creature.

Is Ogopogo a myth or reality? Like "Nessie," the existence of Ogopogo is something you must decide for yourself!

When you care to take a break from your sea monster searching, Okanagan is a haven for summer swimming, sailing, water-skiing, and windsurfing. In the spring and fall before the water has warmed up or cooled down, large rainbow and lake trout are commonly caught in the expansive lake. So, there is a lot more than just Ogopogo to attract you to the deep-blue waters of British Columbia! For more information, call the Okanagan Similkameen Tourism Association at (604) 769–5959.

The Oldest City in Canada

The oldest settlement in Canada is an easy step across the Atlantic Ocean without leaving North America. Quebec City, high atop a 300-foot cliff overlooking the Saint Lawrence River, is the only fortified city on the continent. It is full of historic buildings and winding, narrow streets reminiscent of European architecture.

The city of Quebec was settled by French discoverer Samuel de Champlain in 1608. Champlain found the site a perfect location to establish a fortress which he believed would be impregnable. The first building he constructed was a trading post, and the new colony began to grow around it. The city, first settled by the French, was invaded by the British in the eighteenth century. The medieval-style granite and sandstone wall surrounding Vieux-Québec (Old Quebec) built from 1820–1832 makes it the only walled city north of Mexico.

In the summer of 1759 the city was besieged by the British led by General James Wolfe. Quebec was defended by a young French general, the Marquis de Montcalm. A long series of battles took place in the area until the final battle on the Plains of Abraham when the French army was defeated in less than fifteen minutes. The French were forced to retreat and officially surrendered Quebec to the British Crown when they signed the Treaty of Paris in 1763.

Soon, the British were threatened by Americans during the American Revolution when Americans wished to strike against the British on Canadian soil. In 1775, an army led by American General Benedict Arnold attempted to defeat the British, but were beaten in the last battle to take place in the city.

There are still several reminders of the long conflict between the French and the British within the wall, such as the Citadelle, several historic British towers, and a battlefield park that all remain and are open to the public. Construction began on the Citadelle in 1820 and lasted for more than thirty years. It has twenty-five buildings including the Governor-General's residence, the officers mess, the Cap-Diamant redoubt (1693), and five heavily fortified bastions. The star-shaped plan of the Citadelle is characteristic of Vauban fortifications, and the continued presence of the Canadian Twenty-second Regiment (since 1920) makes it the largest fortified group of buildings still occupied by troops in North America. Military tradition continues with a daily changing of the guard and cannon fire during the summer. Grounds are open to the public.

When in the hands of the British, Quebec never ceased its French heritage. Over its four-century history, it retained its original culture, tradition, and most importantly, French, its official language. Radio and television broadcasts are in French yet Quebec is very accommodating to tourists, as both menus and street signs are bilingual.

Native food is heavily influenced by French culture. The restaurants in Quebec are famous throughout the world for their cuisine and atmosphere. Dozens of restaurants and cafés are located in historic buildings (see French Canadian Cuisine on page 54). Here, gourmet dining is unparalleled, charming, and intimate in old-world surroundings. During the warmer seasons, the streets are lined with busy outdoor cafés. Nightlife abounds in bistros and discotheques that stay open until the wee hours of the morning.

The Quartier Petit-Champlain is the oldest district in

Cafés line the Grande Allée, Quebec's main thoroughfare.
(Photo by Carrie Shook)

North America. When Quebec was founded in 1608, this area became a very busy small port, filled with trading posts and elegant residences. Toward the end of the nineteenth century, the district slowly began to lose its popularity and fell into disrepair for nearly a century. Recently, the area was completely renovated and is now a revitalized, quaint riverside village. It is a lively place where you can walk through narrow streets, browse in boutiques, and enjoy street performers.

The Grande Allée, often referred to as the Champs-Elysées of Quebec, is lined with trees, boutiques, and sidewalk cafés and is found just outside the walls of Old Quebec. This thoroughfare dates back to the French regime when the natives used this road (the longest in Quebec), to sell their furs in town. This route, which linked Quebec City to Cap-

Rouge, is now filled with outdoor cafés and bistros, a hot spot where locals and visitors go for dinner, drinks, and entertainment.

Quebec City boasts the largest collection of seventeenth- and eighteenth-century buildings on the continent. Crammed with national monuments, museums, churches, gourmet cafés, and galleries, Quebec is recognized as one of the world's greatest cities. In 1985 it was placed on the prestigious world heritage list by U.N.E.S.C.O. (United Nations Educational, Scientific, and Cultural Organization) and is the only city in North America to join the company of cities such as Jerusalem, Warsaw, Rome, and Cairo.

Once a small village, this historic settlement is now a bustling city. In fact, it is two cities in one: an old city within the wall, and a modern city outside the wall. The best way to see Old Quebec is on foot rather than by car. Begin a visit to the area with a bus or van tour during the morning or afternoon to get a good feel for the city's layout. The guides are very informational and offer tours in both French and English. Another fun way to see the old city is by horse and buggy. You will find several roaming the streets and it is a worthwhile and inexpensive way to explore.

Many French travel from France to vacation here as it is the cradle of French civilization in North America. Quebec City is a welcoming, friendly place, and the hospitality of all Quebecois is easily recognized by visitors.

French Canadian Cuisine

Canada has had many different cultural influences, beginning with the Native Americans, to the immigration of the French and the British invasion. Depending on the province you are visiting of course, you will find a little more of one influence than another but eating out in Canada is a real treat.

Quebec City's streets are filled with quaint outdoor cafés, and boast a number of internationally known restaurants, rating five stars in quality, service, and atmosphere. The restaurants are located in Old Quebec's most historic buildings, some dating back to the seventeenth century!

There are a number of special restaurants where you can immerse yourself in the French culture. One of the most popular restaurants, Gambrinus, offers both French and continental cuisine in an elegant atmosphere with both indoor and outdoor dining. Specialties of the house include a poached salmon in a mustard sauce, a rack of lamb with basil, veal scallopine with scampi, and several other delicacies. You should make reservations, as the restaurant is packed all year round. Located across from the Chateau Frontenac in a building dating back to 1820, it is at 15 rue du Fort in Old Quebec. Call (418) 692–5144 for reservations.

In the Café de la Paix you will see celebrities from around the globe. This is the place to see and to be seen, and to enjoy French cuisine in a intimate candlelight setting. Specialties of the house include a fresh salmon in a light sauce,

The internationally renowned Aux Anciens Canadiens is located in one of Quebec City's oldest buildings, constructed in 1675–76.
(Photo by Carrie Shook)

rabbit in mustard sauce, rack of lamb Provençale, frogs' legs with garlic, quail in cherry sauce, and a romantic chateaubriand for two. The waiters serve a complimentary house liqueur after dinner. Café de la Paix is located at 44 rue Desjardins. For reservations, call (418) 692–1430.

Aux Anciens Canadiens serves traditional French Quebec

cuisine in a historical setting. The restaurant is located in the oldest building in all of Quebec City, the Maison Jacquet. Built in 1675–1676, the site was granted to Francois Jacquet on November 30, 1674 from the nuns of the neighboring Ursuline Convent. Its thick walls, sturdy joints, and cupboards are characteristic of houses constructed during the late seventeenth century. The restaurant acquired its name from the notable Philippe Aubert de Gaspé, author of the novel *Les anciens canadiens,* who lived there from 1815 to 1824. It is rumored that the famous French General Montcalm lived and later died in the house from wounds received during the local battle against the British at the Plains of Abraham in 1759. Amazingly the house has withstood several battles, fires, and other calamities that Old Quebec has suffered over the centuries.

Specialties here are rich foods that a French Quebec grandmother might serve her family during the holidays or important family gatherings. Favorites include French Canadian pea soup, a maple syrup pie, and a Quebec meat pie.

The following recipes, each representing a specialty from one of the renowned restaurants of Quebec, will allow you to create French delicacies in your own kitchen. Light a few candles, open a bottle of wine, and imagine yourself being in one of the romantic cafés of Quebec City.

Quebec Meat Pie of Aux Anciens Canadiens

    1 lb. chopped pork, chilled
    1 medium peeled and chopped potato
    1 small chopped onion
    ¹/₂ tsp. salt
    ¹/₂ tsp. savory
    ¹/₄ tsp. ground celery seeds
    ¹/₄ tsp. ground cloves

$^1/_2$ cup water

$^1/_2$ cup dry breadcrumbs

1 dough for double-crust pie

Grind pork, potato, and onion through medium plate of meat grinder. Transfer to large heavy saucepan. Stir in salt, savory, ground celery seeds, and cloves. Add water and bring to boil. Reduce heat and simmer until water evaporates (about 20 minutes). Stir in crumbs. Cool completely. Preheat oven to 425° F. Roll dough out on lightly floured surface to thickness of $^1/_8$ inch. Cut out two 11-inch rounds. Fit 1 round into 9-inch pie plate. Add filling, spreading evenly. Cover with second round. Seal edges, crimp decoratively. Make 4 1-inch slits on top to allow steam to escape. Bake until crust is golden brown (35 to 40 minutes.) Serve with chutney. Serves 6.

Aux Anciens Canadiens' Maple Syrup Pie

1$^1/_4$ cup brown sugar (light)

$^1/_2$ cup whipping cream

$^1/_3$ cup maple syrup

1 jumbo egg (room temp.)

2 tsp. butter (room temp.)

1 (9 inch) pie shell

Preheat oven to 350° F. Partially cook pie shell for 5 minutes or until slightly brown. Using electric mixer, beat sugar, cream, syrup, egg, and butter in large bowl until smooth. Pour mixture into crust. Bake until crust is golden brown and filling is set (approximately 45 minutes.) Serve at room temperature. Serves 4–6.

Aux Anciens Canadiens' French Canadian Pea Soup "A La Paysanne"

1 lb. dry yellow peas

$^1/_2$ lb. salted fat pork

2$^3/_4$ qts. water

3 medium size chopped onions (very fine)

2 diced carrots

2–3 bay leaves

1 handful chopped celery leaves

1 oz. chopped parsley

1 tsp. savory

Wash the peas well and place in a large saucepan along with all other ingredients. Put on high heat and bring to a boil. Boil for 2 minutes, and remove from heat. Let stand for 1 hour. Heat again to boiling, then reduce flame and simmer for 1 hour, or until peas are well cooked. Serves 4–6.

Filet Mignon aux Fromage Bleu
Gambrinus Restaurant

2 filet mignon steak

8 oz. dry white wine

1 dozen chopped shallots (small onion)

6 oz. blue cheese

8 oz. powdered or homemade brown gravy

1 oz. heavy whipping cream

Sauté chopped onions in wine on low heat until liquid evaporates. Remove from heat and stir in blue cheese. Add brown gravy and whipping cream and place over low heat until mixture is warm. Remove from heat and strain through a colander. Sauté filet mignon in frying pan with butter until done according to taste. Place filets on serving plate and cover with sauce. Serve with sautéed potatoes and fresh cooked vegetables. Serves 2.

The Bed-and-Breakfast Inns
of Quebec City

Poised majestically above the Saint Lawrence River, Old Quebec is surrounded by a stone wall which is a constant reminder of its long history. Inside the walls is a maze of cobblestone streets, vintage homes, and historical buildings. The best way to experience the city is to stay in an "auberge," a bed-and-breakfast inn. Staying in a quaint Quebecois home situated on one of the city's oldest streets is how you can best experience the French-Canadian way of life. There are a number of inns within the walls of Old Quebec that have fascinating histories. The old city is small and its many cafés, boutiques, and historical sights can be found within a few blocks' radius.

The Hôtel le Manoir d'Auteuil is an auberge within a home built in 1835 which was originally the residence of the sheriff of Quebec, William Sewell. The house, which has been carefully refurbished to show off its elaborate original woodwork and marble is located at 49 rue d'Auteuil. Make reservations by calling (418) 694–1173.

The "300 rue Champlain" is a 175-year-old house with a cozy atmosphere and spacious rooms filled with traditional Quebecois furniture. Located between the cliffs of the historic citadel and the magnificent Saint Lawrence River, it is a short walk from many of the city's highlights, including the Château Frontenac and Place Royal. There are only a handful of bedrooms here, so your stay will be private and peaceful. The inn is located at 300 rue Champlain and reservations can be made by calling (418) 525–9826 between 6:30 P.M. and 8:30 P.M.

There are dozens of other auberges recommended by the Quebec City tourist guidebook, available at the tourist bureau in town. Inns are listed according to price range and available services. A stay in a big hotel will seem like any other city, but when you stay in an auberge, you will truly experience Old Quebec!

The Maritime Provinces

Miles and miles of scenic coastal highways, small fishing villages, towering cliffs and blue waters well describe the maritime provinces of Newfoundland, Nova Scotia, Prince Edward Island, and New Brunswick. The provinces of Atlantic Canada have been left virtually untouched by modern times; each province continues to hold on to the traditions and life-style brought by settlers who sailed to Canada from the British Isles.

The geographical, environmental, and cultural range is enormous in Atlantic Canada spanning over 27,200 kilometers (17,000 miles) of coastline. You will discover green hills and valleys, sparkling rivers with excellent fishing, stretches of dark ocean coastline that are only interrupted by picturesque towns and villages in sheltered coves. You will see icebergs floating in the north, although you could swim in the warm Gulf Stream water of the south. There are isolated fishing areas interspersed between sophisticated cities. Where else in North America but Nova Scotia would you expect to hear Gaelic spoken?

You should enjoy the slow-paced, rustic life-style that is offered by the Maritimes. If you stay in a bed-and-breakfast inn, quaint hotel, or on a vacation farm, you will have the opportunity to experience the native life-style and enjoy traditional Canadian cuisine.

Newfoundland/Labrador

The province of Newfoundland is part landmass, and part island. Labrador's population of 600,000 inhabitants is growing fast—the province has the highest birth rate in the nation.

Most of the population, about 560,000, live on the island of Newfoundland. About 150,000 Newfoundlanders live in the capital city, St. John's. The island is 43,000 square miles (112,000 square kilometers) and is separated from Labrador by the Strait of Belle Isle to the north, and the Atlantic Ocean to the south and east. Newfoundland is the most easterly part of North America and is only 1,800 miles (2,880 kilometers) from the coast of Ireland! The island is heavily forested (pulp and paper are staple commodities), but fishing has been the most important industry ever since the island was settled.

Labrador occupies 110,000 square miles (286,000 square kilometers), and borders Quebec on the south and west and the Atlantic Ocean on the north and east. There are 40,000 people living in Labrador, mostly along the coast. The interior of Labrador is a vast wilderness where few have ever set foot.

Only in Newfoundland can you drive into towns with names such as Bumble Bee, Jerry's Nose, Blow Me Down, Too Good Arm, Empty Basket, or Heart's Desire. Though the names of the towns don't sound historical, Newfoundland's discovery long preluded the discovery of the rest of

St. John's, Newfoundland's largest city, is the oldest inhabited fishing port in North America. (Courtesy Department of Development and Tourism/Newfoundland)

the continent. Vikings settled five centuries before Christopher Columbus made his famous voyage. Helge Ingstad, a Norwegian scientist, was the first to find proof of a Viking settlement at the village of L'Anse-aux-Meadows on the northern tip of Newfoundland.

The Vikings settled in Newfoundland around 1000 A.D., but it wasn't until 1497 when Venetian John Cabot "officially" discovered the land. In 1583, Newfoundland was later claimed for England by the adventurer, Sir Humphrey Gilbert, under the reign of Queen Elizabeth I. England realized Newfoundland's great potential as a rich supplier of seafood and as a useful defensive stronghold ("guardian of the Atlantic"), though made no attempt at colonization. There was little development in Newfoundland until the beginning of the nineteenth century, and it wasn't until 1855 that the province established self-government.

There has been a long conflict between Newfoundland and Quebec over the ownership of Labrador. In 1927, the boundary dispute was officially ended. Quebec, however, continues to claim all of Labrador except for a 32-kilometer (20-mile) strip of coastline. Put to a vote in 1948, by a 2

Whale watching is an unforgettable Newfoundland experience.
(Courtesy Department of Development and
Tourism/Newfoundland)

percent margin, Newfoundland, the oldest British colony, became Canada's newest province.

St. John's is the largest city in Newfoundland and the oldest still-inhabited fishing port on the continent. Through the ages, it has grown from a tiny fishing outport to a bustling port community. The city has retained much of its old-world charm, yet it has kept pace with the modern world.

While in St. John's, you must visit Signal Hill, the largest national historic park in all of Canada. It is located high above St. John's on 500-foot cliffs, overlooking the city, harbor, and sea. Here, the last military engagement over the Atlantic coast occurred between the French and the British and several forts still stand today. On December 12, 1901, at the Cabot Tower, a memorial to John Cabot, at Signal Hill, Guglielmo Marconi received the first transatlantic wireless signal. It was this historical event by which the hill was named. The park is open throughout the year and is free of charge.

A short trip via Highway 11 takes you from St. John's to Cape Spear National Historic Park, which is North America's easternmost point of land. It is a desolate but beautiful place that has been weathered by centuries of storms and the sea. Standing on the cliffs overlooking the Atlantic, with the entire continent behind you, is the closest you can get to Europe without leaving North America. Cape Spear's oldest surviving lighthouse was built in 1835, and continuously used until a more modern facility was erected in 1955. Cape Spear was declared a National Historic Park in 1962 and the original lighthouse was restored. Members of the Cantwell family have continued to tend the lighthouse since 1845. The wind at Cape Spear is often blustery; you may want to bring along a jacket or sweater, even on a sunny day.

The waters off Newfoundland offer excellent opportunities for whale watching, which has become a popular tourist activity. The most commonly sighted large whales are

Cape Spear National Historic Park, situated on North America's most easterly point. (Courtesy Department of Development and Tourism/Newfoundland)

the Humpback and the Fin. The area from Holyrood Bay to St. Mary's Bay on the southern portion of the Avalon Peninsula is considered one of the best locations in the world to watch Humpbacks feeding close to shore. The whales can generally be spotted between April and October, although the best season is from mid-June to mid-July. Several commercial tour operators in St. John's and the surrounding area organize whale-watching expeditions, but an alternative is to ask a local fisherman if he could take your party out on the waters for a minimal fee. For a charter service, call Nova Marine Charters which offer two-hour boat tours at (709) 753–1234.

Gros Morne National Park is on the Great Northern Peninsula on the Gulf of Saint Lawrence. Here you will view magnificent secluded lakes and coves—and fjords as awe-

66

some as anything that you're likely to find anywhere this side of Norway. There are lots of moose and black bear, few people, and four-and-a-half miles of splendid hiking. At its peak, you will overlook the waters of the Gulf of Saint Lawrence and have a breathtaking view of Newfoundland.

Of course, one of the main attractions of Newfoundland is the people, especially those who live in the small fishing villages along the coast. Like the Irish, Newfoundlanders are close-knit families and communities, and are extremely friendly to visitors. The people and their magnificient land and ocean make Newfoundland a must place to visit.

The best way to see the province is by driving along the Trans-Canada Highway. You can bring your car via ferry to Newfoundland's Port-aux-Basques on the island of Newfoundland, and drive along the highway encircling the island. You can make frequent stops for fishing, swimming, boating, sight-seeing, and great picnicking along the countryside. If you like to be alone, there are also hundreds of secluded lakes and streams, where you can enjoy peace and harmony. And don't forget to bring your appetite—you'll have many opportunities to purchase home-baked bread and pies, local produce, and fresh fish. The people of Newfoundland are also proud of their handicrafts including colorful hooked rugs, pine furniture, pottery, jewelry, hand-knit woolens, and fishermen's mitts. There are craft outlets in towns and villages throughout the island, as well as in the homes of the artisans.

Explore Newfoundland and Labrador and visit a place that is wild, wonderful, folksy, charming and a step back into time. It is one of the few places in North America that remains untouched—so, come explore this enchanting virgin land. For more information and assistance in planning a vacation at Newfoundland and Labrador, call the Department of Development and Tourism at (800) 563–6353 or (709) 576–2830.

New Brunswick

Doorway to Atlantic Canada, New Brunswick is a province filled with rolling farmland, rugged forests, winding rivers, and craggy, sea-swept shores. It borders Maine on the west, Quebec on the north, and Nova Scotia at the Isthmus of Chignecto and has more than 2,240 kilometers (1,400 miles) of coastline. You will learn about the province and its people when you visit its sleepy villages, historic towns, craft stores, and museums.

Today, most of the people living in the province are descendants of the Acadians, who were expelled from Nova Scotia. With them they brought their French language, religion, and customs that continue to play an essential role in New Brunswick where 35 percent of the population speak French. New Brunswick is the only officially bilingual province in Canada. There are a number of cultures thriving in New Brunswick. New Denmark, for example, is the largest Danish colony in North America, and here Danish dishes are served year-round in the local restaurants. Today over 700,000 inhabitants live in New Brunswick, with the population concentrated in six cities: Saint John, Moncton, Fredericton, Bathurst, Campbellton, and Edmundston.

On any morning in New Brunswick, you can sit on a sunny wharf, surrounded by lobster traps, and listen to gulls and watch fishermen set out in their boats. Or visit one of the most beautiful waterfalls in North America at Grand Falls. Here, you will see a magnificent cascade that has cut a gorge nearly as deep as that of Niagara and you can take a misty walk around its perimeter for a scenic adventure.

The landmass of New Brunswick is over 72,800 square kilometers (28,000 square miles) of which 88 percent is timberland. The province offers excellent fishing and hunting; sportspeople from around the world travel to New Brunswick for its trout, bass, Atlantic salmon, black bear, and deer. Other outdoor activities which are popular here are snow skiing (there are several good ski areas), snowmobiling and in the summer, popular pastimes include golf, wind surfing, tennis, swimming, canoeing, and horseback riding.

New Brunswick is famous throughout the world for its treasures from land and sea. The fishing season thrives all year round, though the fruit and vegetable growing seasons are short. In late January, when the province is covered with ice and snow, holes are cut through the icy rivers, and fishermen catch fish that are immediately frozen as they are pulled out of the water. The lobster season is a year-round industry except for two short periods in July and October. Crab and herring are the most common types of seafood caught in the province's waters.

The maple sugar season begins during the springtime, and the middle of May brings two delicacies. One is fiddleheads, the unopened heads of the ostrich fern, which are picked just as they emerge from the ground. These are served in many ways: in soups and quiches, marinated, or served with butter or vinegar. The second delicacy, rhubarb, grows everywhere in New Brunswick.

A popular activity in the province is picking your own produce. This is the ideal way to find the freshest fruits and vegetables. U-Pick farms throughout the province allow visitors to fill baskets with unlimited berries—anywhere from one quart to enough to fill a freezer. You can buy a container from the grower or you can bring your own. During the summer months, strawberries are ripe and raspberry season lasts from the middle of July into August. In August, you can pick blueberries, the main fruit crop of New Brunswick. The majority of blueberries are grown in Charlotte County, where there is one U-Pick in St. David Ridge. Late summer and fall introduces plentiful apple orchards. Early apples like Miltons and Melbas are ripe in August, while September brings McIntosh, Cortland, Lobo, Russet, and numerous other varieties. Most U-Picks for all types of produce are primarily found in the towns of New Denmark, Fredericton, Mouth of Keswick, Jemswg, Minto, Sussex, Lameque, Belledune, River Glade, Robertville, Ripples, Grand Falls, and Young's Cove.

The two most interesting cities in New Brunswick are Fredericton, the capital, and Saint John, its largest city (population 130,000). Both are rich in history, so allow ample time to tour forts, churches, and magnificently restored buildings. A quick stop at city hall will earn you a three-day tourist parking pass, so you won't have to feed any parking meters during your stay. Once in town, you'll find that almost everything is within walking distance. For a hearty walk, hike up the hill to the University of New Brunswick (founded in 1785), the oldest provincial and state university in North America. Christ Church Cathedral is one of the finest examples of Gothic architecture on the continent.

If you're driving between Fredericton and Saint John, take Route 202, which follows the Saint John River. It's about thirty minutes longer than the one-hour drive via Highway 7, but the scenery is well worth the extra time. The port of Saint John, at the confluence of the Saint John River and the Bay of Fundy, is a charming city often compared to both Boston and Baltimore. Stroll down Prince William's Walk for an excellent sampling of late nineteenth-century Victorian architecture. Most importantly, do not forget to visit the Bay of Fundy at high and low tide (see page 105).

Nova Scotia

"Ciad Mile Failte" is what you will hear when you visit Nova Scotia, (Gaelic for "New Scotland"). Its translation is "a hundred thousand greetings." Locals are eager to welcome you to their land of quaint seaside communities, sandy beaches, towering cliffs, and rocky coastline. A sense of isolation experienced by generations of Nova Scotians has had a marked influence on their lives. Their daily existence has a different tempo from the rest of Canada—a one-day-at-a-time attitude prevails. The Nova Scotians have a tremendous pride in their cultural history and their sea environment. The Scot, dressed in a colorful tartan and playing the bagpipe, symbolizes these unusual people. Protestant and Roman Catholic Scots fled their beloved country because of famine and political oppression and settled here in the late-eighteenth and early-nineteenth centuries, and have since had a profound influence on the province.

What is interesting about Nova Scotia is that today, more Gaelic is spoken here than in Scotland. Settled by the Acadians in 1605 at Fort Royal, it was the first settlement north of Florida. Its isolation has helped retain its native language. The Acadians established Nova Scotia's first theater, social club, and even planted the continent's first apple orchard, grain, and dandelions. Today, Nova Scotia is the world's largest exporter of lobsters. Called the birthplace of Canada, Nova Scotia served as its capital until 1749.

Many historians believe that Nova Scotia was discovered by Leif Erickson of Norway in 1001 A.D. when he landed at Yarmouth. However, nomadic Indians inhabited the area for nearly 3,000 years before Erickson's arrival. Over the centuries, the province was settled by six groups including Africans, English, French, German, Irish, and Scottish. John Cabot, an Italian who sailed under the English flag, landed at Cape Breton Island on June 24, 1497, a day that is annually celebrated as the founding day of the province. Upon his discovery, he described Nova Scotia's waters as so "full of fish . . . that one takes them . . . with baskets."

Nova Scotia is a large peninsula with a narrow isthmus linking it to New Brunswick, and is surrounded by four great bodies of water including the Atlantic Ocean, the Bay of Fundy, Northumberland Strait, and the Gulf of St. Lawrence. Nova Scotia is comprised of two geologically different entities, Cape Breton Island and the mainland. Cape Breton Island takes up a third of the land area of Nova Scotia. The highest point of Cape Breton Island reaches 1,747 feet, with spectacular cliffs that tower above the shore. This large island is connected to the mainland by a causeway at the Strait of Canso. Stretching for 380 miles, the maritime province has a rocky 4,280-mile Atlantic coastline and measures 21,425 square miles. It is filled with granite cliffs, colonial towns, large bays, crashing surf, and more than 100 lighthouses protect its shores. The center of Nova Scotia is filled with fertile plains and river valleys, though as you travel across this province, you will never be more than thirty-five miles from the sea. Your fishing options are endless: There are more than 1,000 lakes, 300 trout and salmon streams, and the Northumberland Strait with the warmest water north of the Carolinas.

The capital city of Halifax, the largest city in Nova Scotia, and the first English settlement in Canada (1749), is considered to be one of America's most beautiful and historic cities. As a year-round ice-free port, the city plays an important role in Canada's maritime activities, such as fishing, fish processing, and shipping. Second only to Sydney, Australia, Halifax has the largest natural bay in the world and is a seafood lover's paradise—boasting the most pubs and eateries in the country. Be sure to visit the Citadelle, built in 1749, located a short walk from downtown. Perched atop a large hill, it offers an excellent view of the city. A thirty-minute ferry ride across the bay will take you to Halifax's twin city, Dartmouth, for only thirty-five cents each way. Canada's pride and joy, the *Bluenose II* (an exact replica of the 162-foot racing schooner) also offers rides.

In August, the Buskers, an annual two-and-a-half-week carnival, draws street performers and tourists from around the globe. An audience of over 500,000 flocks here to see who will win the $25,000 grand prize for "Most Entertaining Street Performer." Musicians, jugglers, and magicians from America, Europe, and even New Zealand arrive each year, with routines that make each show seem more spectacular than the last.

All year round, thousands of visitors travel to Nova Scotia to enjoy its parks, forests, cliffs, plateaus, foot trails, and pristine areas of unspoiled land. There are hundreds of historic landmarks, breathtaking seascapes, and wonderful flora and fauna to discover. Nova Scotia offers to visitors clean, fresh spring water, a luxury not easily found in many places around the globe.

There are two national parks in Nova Scotia to explore: Cape Breton Highlands National Park and Kejimkujik National Park. The former is 450 kilometers (280 miles) northeast of Halifax. This 234,882-acre park is 1,750 feet above sea level and offers magnificent seascapes with the Atlantic coast and rolling hills in the background. It lies between the Gulf of Saint Lawrence and the Atlantic Ocean. The park offers excellent fishing, camping, hiking, beaches, and Ingonish Beach is one of the finest eighteen-hole golf courses in all of North America. Also at Ingonish Beach is the Keltic Lodge, Nova Scotia's premier resort. This world-famous lodge is operated by the provincial government and offers excellent accommodations including some of the finest cuisine on Cape Breton Island. It also has a heated saltwater swimming pool, entertainment, and dozens of other activities. Since it is usually booked to capacity several months before the start of the season, it is wise to call in advance. Call (902) 285–2880 for more information.

Kejimkujik National Park is located on the western part of the mainland, about 175 kilometers (109 miles) southwest of Halifax. Kejimkujik is a vast inland area of forest, lakes, streams with an abundance of wildlife. Open throughout the year, it offers camping, hiking, boating, canoeing (rentals available), swimming, fishing, and nature walks. Entry to the park is free of charge.

A unique experience available to visitors is the chance to cohabit with Nova Scotian country people, and to be part of their families. Visitors are invited to stay on a farm, where accommodations and meals are inexpensive. This is the best value going anywhere in the province. You dine at their tables, where you might be served Scottish oatcakes, scones, shortbread, haggis, or French-Acadian rapi-pie, a pork and potato concoction. Also served are homemade soups, fruits and vegetables, fish, shellfish, and hot-from-the-oven pies and bread. Most of the food is fresh daily right from the farm. If you choose, you are welcome to lend a hand and help with the chores. You may participate in both family and local community activities. You are invited to stay for just one night, or for as long as you want, even the entire summer. You can come by yourself, with friends or family, whatever your race, ethnic group, or religion, you will be welcome. This is an unbeatable experience that provides an insider's view of the real Nova Scotia. For more information on the location of the farms, write to the Secretary, Farm and Country Vacation Association, R.R. 3, Centreville, Kings County, Nova Scotia, B0P 1J0.

Discover for yourself that Nova Scotia is considered for good reason to be Canada's ocean playground.

Prince Edward Island

The smallest of Canada's ten provinces is Prince Edward Island (P.E.I.), a compact island gem off the east coast of Canada in the Gulf of Saint Lawrence. The crescent-shaped island is only 224 kilometers (140 miles) long and six to sixty-four kilometers (four to forty miles) wide and is separated from its neighboring mainland provinces, Nova Scotia and New Brunswick by the Northumberland Strait. P.E.I. is a rural province, and the capital, Charlottetown, the only city, has a population of 15,800. This beautiful, rustic island has 500 miles of soft sand beaches and the warmest water north of the Carolinas. You are never very far from the sea, no matter where on the island you may be. Nicknamed the "Garden of the Gulf," the land is so well-manicured, that every town and village looks as if it is a scene from a romantic postcard.

P.E.I. is one of Canada's most densely populated provinces but has a minimal population growth because its younger generation keeps migrating to more industrialized areas in Canada. The current population is 128,000, with the bulk of the population living in the greater Charlottetown area (estimated population is 30,000).

Jacques Cartier discovered P.E.I. for the French in 1534. Cartier was fascinated with the island's color and beauty, describing what he saw from his ship as ". . . the fairest land 'tis possible to see!" In 1719, the first white colonists settled at Port La Joye, now Fort Amherst/Port La Joye National

75

Historic Site, just across the Charlottetown harbor. The island changed hands several times during the wars between Britain and France. By 1758, Britain occupied the island and deported most of the Acadian settlers back to Europe and to Louisiana (where they became known as "Cajuns"). A few remained on the island after escaping expulsion by fleeing to the woods. During British control, the island was divided in 1764 into sixty-seven lots of 20,000 acres each and in a great lottery held in London, wealthy Englishmen drew lots for land grants. A struggle between farmers and absentee landowners occurred, which lasted nearly 100 years. In 1853, the Land Purchase Act authorized the island government to buy back most of the lots for resale to tenants. Twenty years later, all remaining land was purchased and resold by the Government. In 1864, leaders from the Canadian provinces gathered in Charlottetown to discuss a political and economic union of British North America, and P.E.I. became the birthplace of Canada. In 1867, Canada became a nation. In 1873, after mounting railway debts and promises by the federal government of continuous communication with the mainland, Prince Edward Island reluctantly joined the new Canadian nation.

Although P.E.I. is Canada's smallest province, the island has more miles of paved road per capita than any other part of the country. You can see P.E.I. on one of its three scenic drives by automobile, recreational vehicle, or bicycle. The drives will take you from one discovery to the next, from popular attractions to out-of-the-way places, close to nature. The drives vary considerably in length; however, any one of them can be completed by car in a day, depending on the number of stops and side trips made along the way. The Blue Heron Drive is 190 kilometers (120 miles), the Lady Slipper Drive is 288 kilometers (180 miles), and the Kings Byway Drive is 375 kilometers (234 miles) long.

The 2,184 square-mile (567,000 hectares) island is small

enough that you are never far from any attraction and you will never run out of things to do. Water sports available along the island's coast range from boardsailing to deep-sea fishing. Other activities include horseback riding, camping, harness racing, amusement parks, festivals, repertory theater, and fantastic lobster suppers!

Fringed by the Gulf of Saint Lawrence, the Prince Edward Island National Park has some of the finest white-sand beaches in North America. The park is a forty-kilometer stretch of sand, bluffs, salt marshes, and freshwater ponds. Although it is one of Canada's smallest national parks, more than 500,000 tourists visit annually to sun, swim, and explore. In the park near Cavendish, you will enjoy magnificent pink beaches filled with sand tinted by the erosion of bleached red clay.

The island is also known for its many vacation farms where you can help earn your keep by doing chores with your host family. You will enjoy home-cooked meals and pleasant, homey accommodations. This is a great way to become acquainted with the life-style of the locals and is an inexpensive alternative to a more expensive hotel room. For a list of farms, call the P.E.I. Department of Tourism and Parks at (800) 565–9060 and (902) 368–4444, if you are east of the Mississippi.

For more information about Prince Edward Island, call (800) 565–7421 while in the Maritimes, (800) 565–0243 from Ontario, Quebec, and Newfoundland, and (800) 565–9060 from the eastern United States.

Anne of Green Gables

Prince Edward Island owes a lot to a fictitious heroine with long red braids. In 1895, author L. M. Montgomery jotted down on a piece of paper: "Elderly couple apply to orphan asylum for a boy. By mistake a girl is sent them." Ten years later, Montgomery came across her story idea again and developed it into a classic children's series, *Anne of Green Gables.*

In the pastoral, storybook setting of Prince Edward Island, the lovable heroine, Anne, has won the hearts of millions with her sense of loyalty and ability to be an independent thinker and free spirit in a strict society. The *Anne* series has been translated into forty languages, and has spawned a musical, two Hollywood films, and two successful television miniseries. This young heroine has helped make Prince Edward Island a mecca to over 700,000 visitors a year.

Two films made in 1934 and 1940 starring Anne Shirley (a.k.a. Dawn O'Day) are still featured on the late, late shows. On prime-time television, Canadian actress Megan Follows is Anne to millions of fans. The television miniseries has aired in forty-one countries and is also a classic. Anne's legend is reborn every summer at the Confederation Centre for the Arts in Charlottetown. Since July 27, 1965, a live theater production of *Anne of Green Gables* has been packing the house. The musical is held from June through October. Call the arts center at (902) 566–2464 for more information.

On P.E.I., *Anne* fans can explore the locations where the heroine's adventures took place. Montgomery used real places she discovered in her own life settings in the *Anne* books. For example, the real Green Gables House, a simple white-and-green farmhouse in Cavindish was once the home of Montgomery's cousins, the MacNeills. Nearby are Anne's favorite places: the Haunted Wood, Lover's Lane, and Babbling Brook. Located on Route 6, Green Gables offers free admission and is open daily, May through October, from 9 A.M. to 5 P.M. (open until 8 P.M. from mid-June to Labor Day). For more information call (902) 672–2211.

The "House of Dreams" where Anne and Gilbert spent their early days as newlyweds is also open to the public. Located in the French River area on Route 20, it is furnished with turn-of-the-century antiques. Hours are 10 A.M. to 4 P.M. daily from June through October (open until 8 P.M. during July and August). Call (902) 886–2098 for more information.

Maud Montgomery's birthplace in New London displays the wedding dress the author wore in 1911 and personal scrapbooks containing copies of her many poems and stories. It is open daily from June through the first half of September from 9 A.M. to 6 P.M. (open until 8 P.M. during July and August). Hours from the last half of September to Thanksgiving are 10 A.M. to 5 P.M. daily. Call (902) 886–2596 for more information.

The Yukon

The Yukon began for one reason: gold. When prospector George Washington Carmack discovered gold on August 16, 1896, it marked the beginning of the Klondike Gold Rush, the world's biggest ever. From this date on, the Yukon was transformed from an uncharted wilderness to the site of some of the most exciting and wild times in North American history.

Like wildfire, the cry of "gold" was heard from Alaska south to Seattle. Soon thereafter, the word spread around the world. In 1897, a steamer pulled into the port at Seattle filled with nearly three tons of gold dust and nuggets from the Klondike creeks, making even nonbelievers take heed.

Worldwide economic times were strained during the late nineteenth century. It's no wonder that by 1898, it seemed as if everyone and his dog was headed for the Klondike. Thousands were lured to the Yukon from faraway places such as Germany and Switzerland; the dream of sudden riches brought over 100,000 determined prospectors who let nothing stop their insatiable appetite. Half of the battle was just getting there.

The greatest barrier between the adventuresome fortune seekers and their pot of gold was the legendary Chilkoot Pass. The entranceway to the territory required climbing treacherous ice steps cut into a nearly vertical cliff. To save lives, the North-West Mounties had passed a law limiting prospectors to carrying only a year's worth of supplies, 907 kilograms (2,000 pounds) over the pass. The dangerous journey took several weeks, often running into months, depending on weather conditions. Tombstones mark the paths of those who didn't survive.

Once gold diggers passed the Chilkoot, Bennett Lake awaited, where they cut down trees to build boats for their crossing. Beyond the lake was the Yukon River, one of the ten biggest waterways in the world, nicknamed the "Highway to the Klondike." While navigating the river, the gold seekers had to pass Miles Canyon, a dangerously narrow passageway leading to a tricky whirlpool. Next came the White Horse Rapids, so named because its rough waves resembled the flowing manes of white stallions. By May 29, 1898, an estimated 7,000 crafts of every shape and size had survived the journey. Onward they floated, past a large Indian community called Carmacks, named after the man who discovered the gold. Then, they traveled past the Five Finger Rapids to the town of Dawson.

Yukon, ho! (Courtesy Tourism Yukon)

The Klondike Highway offers a spectacular view of the Yukon.
(Courtesy Tourism Yukon)

As if out in the middle of nowhere, Dawson sprang up to become the biggest and trendiest town west of Winnipeg. A bar stood on every corner, each having its own legendary "Klondike Kate," the fact-based patroness of local establishments. During the peak of the rush, the boomtown's population soared to over 30,000. Today, many of its original buildings still stand, including the Eldorado Hotel, as described in Jack London's *Call of the Wild*. London's own cabin still stands in the downtown area. Many of the buildings have been restored and offer guided tours.

The famous Yukon gold rush lasted only ten years. By 1903, over $96 million in gold was mined from the Klondike, though millionaires were few. Today, gold is still on the minds of many who mine with modern equipment. Thanks to modern transportation the Yukon is more accessible. The tortuous rapids of yesterday and the forbidding canyons are now tamed into great vacation areas.

The territory's gold fever is still contagious. Ride the historic White Pass train. Packed with history, the antiquated railway that once linked the goldfields to the outside world now operates as a fun-filled passenger service, with "parlor" cars built in the 1800s. The journey takes you past the "Gold Rush Cemetery," the burial grounds of famous gold rushers, but the real highlight is the magnificent panoramic view. Round-trip excursions are available from Skagway with through connections to Whitehorse, capital city of the Yukon. For reservations or more information about the White Pass train, call (800) 343–7373 or (907) 983–2217. For more information on the Yukon, call (403) 667–5340.

Only in the Cariboo

The Cariboo is the "Texas of British Columbia," an expansive land with a long history. The province has enjoyed a successful cattle business which still plays a major role in its economy, in the tradition similar to the American west. Cariboo cattlemen operate some of the largest ranches in the world.

Ranches open to guests are scattered across the land, through the lake country and into rugged mountain valleys. You will find ranches catering only to children while others are for the entire family to enjoy. Rural hospitality, hearty ranch meals, plenty of fresh air, and lots of exercise will do wonders for your spirit.

Some ranches offer pack trips into the highlands. You can ride on part of the historic Mackenzie Trail where, in 1793, the explorer Alexander Mackenzie became the first person to cross North America by land. Riders can explore the rugged mountains and massive lakes of this big country. Pack trips generally last from three to ten days, although some are even longer. The length of the trip is based on your personal endurance and experience. A variety of rides are offered, including photographic- and naturalist-oriented ones. You may even choose a combination trip that includes fishing, canoeing, and river rafting. The ranches can be visited year-round. You can cross-country ski in the winter or enjoy swimming and boating in the summer. Fishing is a year-round activity.

If you decide to stay on a working cattle ranch, a dude ranch, or an outfitter, you have dozens of activities to choose from. If you want to go by horseback, there are short-trail rides and experienced guides to lead you. Perhaps a hayride is more your style! At night after a western-style meal, you will enjoy a sing-along, or an old-fashioned, foot-stomping square dance. So grab a partner, and join the fun.

A stay on a real cattle ranch or a pack trip is an ideal way to understand and enjoy the great Canadian west. There are hundreds of miles of unexplored wilderness just waiting to be discovered and many ghost towns and abandoned gold mines that testify to Canada's colorful past. No wonder it is called the "Big Country."

Bracewell's Alpine/Wilderness Adventures is a wilderness ranch resort in Tatlayoko Lake, just about as far from civilization as you can get. The 10,000 square-foot log ranch house has rooms with mountain views and includes hearty country cooking in the dining room, with a variety of packages for short or long visits. For more information, call (604) 372–2338.

The Top of the World Guest Ranch is a 40,000-acre working cattle ranch, located in the Canadian Rockies, about an hour's drive from Banff National Park. The ranch accommodates only thirty guests and features comfortable log cabins with ranch-style meals. Call (604) 426–6303 for reservations and information.

When you make reservations, the ranches will tell you what to bring. It is always fun to play the part, so be sure to bring your cowboy boots and hat along. If you don't own either of these standard items, you can usually rent or purchase them at the ranch. A visit to a ranch is perfect for those longing for adventure and wide-open spaces.

Freshwater Fishing in British Columbia

British Columbia is snowcapped mountains, evergreen rain forests, and rugged coastlines. It is also a vast land filled with farms, lush orchards, sprawling prairie plains, grassy plateaus, boreal forests, and a collection of hundreds of offshore islands, one of which (Vancouver Island) is larger than nine U.S. states. British Columbia, with thousands of clear lakes and rivers from which to choose, can practically offer each fisherman his own. The waters are rich with fish, and depending on the area of the province you visit, there is a wide variety of game for fishing fanatics.

If you are a fly-fisher, you will find the lakes of British Columbia custom-made for fly casting. Use a floating or neutral-sink line in May and June when the sea life is just hatching, a sinking line used in July and August for catching mature fish in deeper waters. Rainbow trout is the most sought-after fish, and Kokanee salmon is the next most popular. They are primarily found in the larger lakes and are usually caught with bright spinners with worms or with small fluorescent lures.

The biggest game fish of British Columbia is the sturgeon. King Henry I forbade the consumption of sturgeon at any other table in the kingdom than his own. His order became law and still remains on the books to this day. Later, this caviar-carrying fish was decreed a "royal fish" by King Edward II.

Record-weight white sturgeon have been caught in the Fraser River. The largest on record was caught in lower Fraser over fifty years ago, measuring almost six meters (twenty feet) and weighing 832 kilograms (1,832 pounds). The fish was estimated to be 100 years old. The sturgeon of the upper river tend to be somewhat smaller, weighing between eighteen and twenty-four kilograms (sixty to eighty pounds). Fish weighing 225 to 360 kilograms (500 to 800 pounds) have been reported in the Lillooet area of the river.

Cariboo country offers over 8,000 lakes of all sizes to choose from and a variety of drive-in lodges and remote fly-in camps (lakeside areas only reachable by hydroplane) that provide accommodations. Here, pan-fry rainbow and brook trout are among the most popular catch of the day. When you take a break from fishing, other activities to explore include river rafting, canoeing, horseback riding, hiking, gold panning, or just plain relaxing. For assistance in planning a trip, call Coho Fishing Adventures at (604) 324–8214, or in the U.S., call (800) 663–8755. They can offer suggestions regarding accommodations, renting equipment, transportation, etc.

Few places in the world other than British Columbia offer such an abundance and variety of good fishing in such beautiful and unspoiled natural surroundings. It is a place where prizewinning fish and spectacular alpine scenery await you. See for yourself, and bring sturdy fishing gear! For information, brochures, and rates on freshwater-fishing resorts in British Columbia, write Sport Fishing Information Center, P.O. Box 9595, Vancouver, B.C., Canada, V6B 4G3.

Rail Across Canada

There is little more exciting or adventurous than a three-day, 2,887-mile long rail journey across the broad expanse of Canada. From the Pacific to the Atlantic, or east to west, you will see the untamed western life-style of British Columbia and the French sophistication of Montreal. Your train will stop for a moose on the tracks; slow to a hush so as not to cause an avalanche; and hold a grand game of bingo while waiting for a rockslide to be cleared away.

More and more people are re-discovering the comforts and luxuries afforded by traveling by train. The train blends in as part of the scenery, and puts you right in the middle of things, rather than as a passerby traveling by car or bus.

The "Canadian," the V.I.A. Rail, glides across Canada along the same routes taken by early explorers. The train runs along the tops of tall mountains, passes by the sides of deep chasms, and crosses great waters. You will see the prairie country, a vast area where the land never seems to end, that provides grain to Canada, China, Africa, and the Soviet Union. When you awake in the morning, as the train enters Ontario, you will be greeted with the rocky shore of Lake Superior and on to Toronto. In little more than four hours, you will arrive in Montreal.

The Canadian is an air-conditioned, luxury vehicle that allows you to forget about all the hassles of driving and finding accommodations. In addition to regular coach service, you can book accommodations in a sleeping car. Bedrooms have an upper and lower bed, with a private bathroom. Another option is a roomette, that offers a bed for one person and private bath. There is also a section that has deep-cushioned seats for day travel, equipped with an upper and lower berth for night use. In the morning, you can wake up to hot coffee and fresh donuts aboard the Dome car, a railroad car crowned by a transparent bubble, providing an incredible view.

The V.I.A. Rail is a crown corporation that was established by the Canadian parliament. Almost ten years ago, the two major railways, Canadian National and Canadian Pacific were in desperate need of a face-lift; equipment was deteriorating, layoffs and terminations lowered employee morale, and the cars only serviced several necessary but unprofitable stops between remote towns and trading centers. Under Pierre Trudeau, the longest-serving prime minister in Canada's history, both railways were consolidated and services were improved.

Sir William Van Hornes, the guiding force behind the railroad's construction in the nineteenth century, summed it up this way, "Since we cannot export the scenery, we shall have to import the tourists." Canada has been doing that ever since.

Traveling across Canada aboard the "Canadian" is a less expensive option than air travel from coast to coast. The least expensive option is a fifteen-day-long pass, which allows you to use the train at your leisure for over two weeks. V.I.A. Rail also operates several package tours that may include rental cars, hotels, and air transportation. You are encouraged to make reservations ahead of time. For reservations or more information about rates and packages, write Manager, Customer Service Development, V.I.A. Rail Canada, P.O. Box 8116, 2 Place Ville-Marie, Montreal, Quebec, H3B 2G6, Canada, or call (514) 871–1331 or (800) 561–3949.

Canada's Mountain Playgrounds

The largest mountain parkland in the world is comprised of Canada's four contiguous Rocky mountain parks, Banff, Yoho, Kootenay, and Jasper. Each park is a separate entity, totaling over 7,800 square miles of national park area. The boundaries drawn between the parks are artificial, though natural features give each of these parks its own unique character. The parks contain nearly 2,000 miles of trails, providing one of the best hiking areas in North America. Within the parks is the highest waterfall in Canada, the largest icefield in the Rocky Mountains, and a wide array of plant and animal species.

Hundreds of types of wildlife live within the park including grizzly bears, bison, elk, mule deer, moose, bighorn sheep, mountain goats, and more than 200 species of birds. Waterfowl is also abundant, such as ducks, grebes, swans, and geese, who use the lakes of the park for resting stops on migratory routes.

The four parks contain three towns, one village, two golf courses, four swimming pools, four downhill-ski areas, thirty-two campgrounds, twenty-one backcountry lodges and huts, twenty-nine commercial lodges, and more than 350 miles of major highways. So, there are several amenities throughout the four parks for those of you who don't want to "rough it." The towns of Banff and Jasper, within their namesake parks, contain hotels, motels, restaurants of every kind, and many tourist services from boat rentals to trail-ride stables. In addition, there are several lodges on beautiful lakes throughout the parks, including the Moraine Lodge and Cabins and the famous Chateau Lake Louise. The parks have become a tourist mecca, where visitors can view the spectacular scenery of the mountain playground in high style.

The Trans-Canada Highway is the primary east-west route through the Canadian Rockies. The highway enters Banff park via Bow Valley, follows past the villages of Banff and Lake Louise, to the summit of the Kicking Horse Pass, and descends through the heartland of Yoho National Park via the Kicking Horse Valley. The distance from East Banff to West Yoho is 80.3 miles, and this highway is, in fact, the only road that traverses Yoho Park. Providing excellent views of the valley and surrounding peaks, all points of interest in the park can be reached from various trails and roads off the main highway. Traffic passes through the highway at high speeds; many cars and trucks are merely passing through the Rockies on their way to other destinations, so be prepared to pull over at pull-offs and picnic areas to catch the good views. There is a better, more leisurely and scenic alternative No. 1 Highway which parallels the Trans-Canada Highway for most of the way throughout the park.

The highway crests the backbone of the Rockies in an area known as the "Great Divide." Here, all waters east of this point flow into the Saskatchewan River system and eventually into the Hudson Bay. Waters flowing west empty into the Columbia River and Pacific Ocean. There is a pull-off that is an excellent place to stop to view the rugged mountainous region. The Great Divide is the boundary between Alberta and British Columbia, and also separates Banff from Yoho National Park.

The Yoho Valley Road Junction, an eight mile-long side road, stretches to some of the best features of Yoho Park. This eight-mile strip offers incredibly tight switchbacks that will lift you well above the floor of the valley in less than a half-mile. The road continues through an area where avalanches have swept down, clearing trees from their paths, leaving the lumber in piles on the valley floor. At the top of the road is the Takkakaw Falls, the highest waterfall in Canada. The falls "thunder" off a towering cliff of limestone, and drop 1,248 feet to the valley floor. Beyond the falls is an excellent hiking trail that reaches the uppermost points of Yoho. Cathedral Mountain Chalets offer accommodations, groceries, and gasoline during the summer season. There are also campgrounds along Yoho Valley Road. Scenic views and trails are well marked.

Banff is the oldest and largest of the townsites within the mountain parks, undoubtedly owing its existence to the discovery of hot mineral springs on the slopes of nearby Sulphur Mountain. In 1885, the springs were believed to have "great sanitary advantage to the public," so the Canadian government proclaimed the area a nature preserve. Soon, the area was expanded to include over 260 square miles and was designated as the Rocky Mountains National Park, the first national park in the country. Today, the town of Banff is home to over 4,000 year-round inhabitants.

Lake Louise of Banff National Park owes its name to Princess Louise Caroline Alberta, wife of the Marquis of Lorne, governor-general of Canada from 1878 to 1883. In the 1890s, the lake was a hub for exploration and adventure in the Rockies. Mountaineers from all over the world traveled here to scale the unclimbed summits surrounding the lake, and to explore the northern untracked valleys leading to the Columbia Icefield. The lake has a unique greenish-blue color and sits 5,680 feet above sea level in the zone of subalpine forest.

Kootenay National Park was established in 1920 when the Banff-Windermere Parkway was built, the first roadway across the central Rockies from Alberta to British Columbia. The sixty-five-mile-long drive was constructed by the federal government in exchange for a strip of land (from British

Columbia) five miles wide on either side of the highway to use as a national park, later named Kootenay. This drive is one of the most scenic routes in the mountain parks and is the only way to enter Kootenay National Park by car.

Vermillion Pass, at 5,416 feet above sea level is the summit of the Great Divide and serves as a boundary between Banff and Kootenay parks. Here, there is a self-guided nature walk called the Fireweed Trail that leads through a portion of the pass where, in the summer of 1968, fires burned across 6,000 acres for four days. This is an excellent opportunity to view a fire-ravaged forest close up, and witness how life goes on as wildlife continues to exist in the still-charred area. The trail gets its name from the common wildflower found here, fireweed, a plant that grows wherever the landscape has been disturbed by either fire or man.

Radium Hot Springs in Kootenay offers pools of spring water with temperatures ranging from 35 degrees C. to 47 degrees C. (95 degrees F. to 117 degrees F.), depending on the season of the year. The springs are named Radium Hot Springs due to their relatively high radioactivity. The water is heated several thousand feet below the earth's surface and percolated upward to appear in the form of hot springs. Here, there is a hot pool, swimming pool, bathhouse, lodge, and a restaurant.

The Icefield Parkway is another exceptional roadway in the Canadian Rockies. This parkway is the longest tour within the four parks, stretching 145 miles from the Trans-Canada Highway to the town of Jasper. The Icefield Parkway follows along the Great Divide in a north-south direction and crests two passes, Bow Summit (6,787 feet) and Sunwapta (6,675 feet) which are the highest traversed by traffic in the parks. All terrain viewed along the parkway have been heavily glaciated, with over 100 glaciers still visible from the road between Jasper and Lake Louise. As the road winds, you'll see gigantic glaciers draped in white-blue folds from summits high above including the Athabasca Glacier, a large area of the 100 square-mile Columbia Icefield that is part of the largest body of ice in the Rockies, accessible by road. Here, you will view mountains that rise 12,000 feet above sea level. You will see idyllic lakes that mirror the great mountains and an unmitigated wilderness with a silence only broken by the rush of waterfalls and the thunder of distant avalanches. This parkway is also famous for close up views of wildlife.

The Yellowhead Highway, also known as Route 16 and the Jasper-Edmonton Highway, is the main road running east-west through Jasper National Park. A relatively short route, the road is 48.5 miles long and passes through the shores of Jasper Lake, the town of Jasper and the old fur trade outpost of Jasper's House.

Located on the banks of the Sulphur Creek in Jasper National Park is the Miette Hot Springs, the warmest in the Canadian Rockies. The hottest temperatures reach 54 degrees C. (129 degrees F.) with an estimated 250,000 gallons of fresh water erupting daily from the springs. The hot springs are known for their extremely high calcium content, the most found anywhere in the Rockies. Here, you can enjoy a pool and bathing facilities, campgrounds, a resort motel, a grocery store, and a restaurant.

One of the best ways to see Canadian Rockies national parks is by foot, along one of the hundreds of trails. There are more than 2,000 miles of trails that range from short hikes to extended treks of more than one hundred miles. Off-trail travelers must register with park wardens, and must also obtain a permit to build open fires in the backcountry. If you happen to visit the parks during the colder months, you may have a tour of the park aboard a horse-pulled sleigh. By foot, sleigh, bicycle, canoe, horse, or car, any way you choose to see the Canadian Rockies is an adventure.

Canada's Icy Wilderness Park

Unsurpassed among Canada's parks system for wilderness on a grand scale, Kluane National Park Reserve is a realm of over 200 glaciers, tall mountains, alpine meadows, dense forests, and frozen rivers. The park, just a few miles from the Pacific Ocean, fills the Yukon Territory's southwest corner that lies between British Columbia and Alaska. The ice age lives on at Kluane; much of the park is covered by a half-mile-thick sheet of ice. Kluane is one of the newest and largest of all the untouched parks in Canada.

Kluane is over 8,500 square miles of remote and pristine wilderness territory and encompasses the St. Elias Mountains. At nearly 20,000 feet above sea level, this is the highest range of mountains in North America (surpassed only by the summit of Alaska's Mount McKinley). Between the snow-crowned heads of St. Elias is the largest subpolar icefield system outside of Greenland. Here, brave explorers endure some of the world's harshest and coldest weather conditions. Ten of St. Elias' peaks exceed 15,000 feet. Mount Logan, the highest mountain peak in Canada, towers 19,524 above sea level.

There is a rich and varied wildlife living in the park, with over 106 species of birds, including eagles, falcons, and hawks, as well as Dall sheep, mountain goats, timber wolves, grizzly bears, black bears, and moose.

More than 60,000 travelers from all over the world visit the park each year, usually during the warmer months of

June to October. You must register with the park wardens before you explore the backcountry. This is for your own safety since unexpected snowstorms and rising rivers sometimes make the backcountry a trap to hikers. The longest and one of the most popular trails is "Cottonwood," a horseshoe-shaped fifty-mile route. It's quite a hike, but well worth the effort. (Experienced hikers only, please.)

Kluane also attracts a few avid cross-country skiers who brave the cold weather from December through April. Daring mountaineers who climb the high peaks of the park generally do so in the spring and early summer.

The park borders the United States' Wrangell-St. Elias National Park in Alaska. Both parks are recognized by U.N.E.S.C.O. as a joint world-heritage site. Pull on your boots, pack your woolens and enjoy one of the great parks of the world!

The Great White Polar Bear

Once a year in Churchill, Manitoba, some unusual visitors take a leisurely stroll through the town. Located on the rocky coast of the Hudson Bay about a thousand miles north of Winnipeg, the town plays host to great white polar bears who drop in during the fall migrating season and roam freely through the streets. Male bears weigh in at about 1,000 pounds, and females tip the scales at 500 pounds, so these bears wander wherever they choose. Appropriately enough, they are called "The Lords of the Arctic."

The bears stick around only until ice forms on the bay enabling them to hunt for seals. However, when the passing freshwater of the Churchill River freezes earlier than the salty waters of the Hudson Bay, the bears stay longer and search the town for food.

As majestic as the bears look, they are extremely dangerous. Having no natural enemies, they fear nothing and are not easily frightened away. While delightful to watch, you must keep your distance—under no circumstances should you ever attempt to pet a polar bear. The townspeople have learned to live with these imposing guests; a polar bear alert system warns residents of any visit.

Each year brings thousands of tourists to this friendly village of about 1,800 residents. This is the world's only easily-accessible human habitat where polar bears can be seen in their natural environment.

One of Churchill, Manitoba's annual visitors.
(Courtesy Travel Manitoba)

Niagara Falls

In what Canadian spot would you expect to find honeymooners, stuntmen, and tourists by the hundreds? Only at Niagara Falls, one of the natural wonders of the world. The falls are incredible—ton after ton of rushing water thunders down into the Niagara River.

The falls dwarf everything else in sight. The Canadian Horseshoe Falls are 176 feet high and 2,200 feet across. The straight-crested American Falls are 1,000 feet across and 184 feet high. A little known fact is that the falls are moving back due to erosion, but at a sporadic rate. Sometimes the limestone ledges break off, causing large rockfalls, but this is infrequent. The most recent rockfalls occurred at the American Falls in 1931, 1946, and 1956. The American Falls erode a few inches a year, while the Canadian Falls lose over three feet annually because they carry approximately 95 percent of the water from the Niagara River.

Each year, thousands of honeymooners flock to the falls from all over the world. This tradition, which is now a cliché, stems from an old legend that Napoleon's brother traveled by stagecoach from New Orleans to the falls for his honeymoon. This honeymoon started a tradition that has continued since the early nineteenth century.

Located one minute from the falls is the Niagara Falls Museum, the oldest museum in North America. It offers twenty-six galleries featuring several different kinds of exhibits. The museum was founded in 1827 and has been visited by some of the most important figures in history including King Edward VII, Abraham Lincoln, Ulysses S. Grant, and P. T. Barnum. The highlight of the museum is the Daredevil Hall of Fame which offers exhibits about daredevils who have attempted to challenge the falls with a variety of stunts. Once you see how big the falls are, you will be amazed to hear about the various stunts people have attempted! Tightropes, barrels, boats, and rubber balls are on display. Who in their right mind would go down the falls inside a rubber ball?

Another exhibit features the Great Blondin, the falls' most celebrated daredevil. Jean-Francois Gravelet, a Frenchman, was the first person to walk on a tightrope across the Niagara Gorge, in 1859. He crossed several times, often carrying his manager on his shoulders. Gravelet made the daring trip while preparing a meal, riding a bicycle and even blindfolded!

The first successful trip over the Niagara Falls was made by a plump schoolteacher on October 24, 1901. The pride of the continent, Ms. Annie Taylor was pulled from her historic barrel some three hours after it had been loosed in the Upper River. Jean Lussier made his famous plunge on July 4, 1928 in a rubber ball he designed. He had seen his predecessors' fates and designed an airtight ball that was both stable and flexible. His device was completely coated in rubber and held forty hours' worth of oxygen stored in canisters. This trip over the falls was successful and for many years he sold autographs and souvenir scraps of rubber to his fans who visited the museum. Both Taylor's barrel and Lussier's rubber ball are on display in the museum. Hours during the summer from 8:30 A.M. to 11 P.M. daily. During the winter, the museum is only open during weekends and for scheduled tours. Call (416) 356–2151 in Canada and (716) 285–4898 in the United States for more information.

You can see the falls from many different angles, from top

The Maid of the Mist, *on display at the Niagara Falls Museum.*
(Photo by Wayne Farrar/courtesy Niagara Falls Museum)

to bottom. The famous *Maid of the Mist*, a fleet of three small diesel-powered boats, will take you to the front of the American Fall and then upriver right into the horseshoe of the main falls. This is perhaps the best way to see the falls and the provided raingear is a must. The boats are named after a legendary Indian woman who is said to have fallen over the edge of the falls in her small canoe. Some say they see her ghost in the spray. This historic boat ride dates back to the mid-nineteenth century. The first *Maid of the Mist* steamboat began ferrying passengers across the river below the falls in 1846. President Theodore Roosevelt described this trip as "the only way to fully realize the grandeur of the Great Falls of Niagara." The *Maid of the Mist* tour has continued to delight millions of tourists including the famous Nehru in 1949, Marilyn Monroe who filmed the movie *Niagara* in 1953, and Soviet Premier Alexei N. Kosygin who took the classic tourist trip in 1967. It is open daily from mid-May to mid-October and is located at 5920 River Road. Call (416) 358–5781 for more information.

The Minolta Tower Center has high-speed elevators that whisk visitors to heights 203 meters (665 feet) above the falls where there are dining facilities with a spectacular view. It is located at 6732 Oakes Drive and is open daily all year. The "Great Gorge Trip" is an elevator ride that takes visitors to a walkway below the falls that runs along Niagara's edge to the Whirlpool Rapids. It is located at 4330 River Road and is

The Maid of the Mist *tour gives the best view of the falls.* (Courtesy Maid of the Mist)

open from May through October. The Niagara Spanish Aero Car, a cable car, takes passengers up a dizzying climb of 549 meters (1,800 feet) high above the whirlpool of the rapids. The cable car is located at the Niagara Parkway at the Rapids. It is open from mid-April to mid-October, daily. Niagara Helicopters fly over the falls and offer a spine-tingling bird's-eye view. Niagara Helicopters Ltd. is located at 3751 Victoria Avenue near the Whirlpool Rapids, and is open daily all year, weather permitting. The falls can also be enjoyed indoors by visiting the Table Rock Scenic Tunnels that provide tours from points behind the falls through rock-cut tunnels. Raincoats are also provided on this tour. The tunnels are at the Queen Victoria Park at the falls, and are open daily, year round. From any angle, the power and magnificence of the falls will inspire you.

At the brink of the Horseshoe Falls is the location of the forty-six-ton American side-wheeler *Caroline* which was destroyed in the early nineteenth century. A group of rebels living on Navy Island with a newly established provisional government were using the ship to hold supplies. Royal Navy Captain Andrew Drew and a group of volunteers crossed the river, cut the ship loose, and set it afire. The ship ran aground and burned on the edge of the falls.

The falls are reported to be the site for the best water-power development in the entire world. In order to save the falls' scenic beauty, the governments of the United States and Canada signed a treaty in 1950 limiting the two countries to sharing equally a specified amount of water (which falls at a rate of 130,000 cubic feet per second). The electricity generated serves a large industrial area, including Buffalo, Niagara Falls, N.Y., and much of Ontario.

Niagara Falls are spectacular both in winter and summer. There is a wonderful light display that completely illuminates the falls each night all year round. By day, you are bound to spot rainbows in Niagara's mist.

Tremendous Tides

Twice each day, an incredible one-hundred billion tons of water journey up the shores of the Bay of Fundy in New Brunswick. To be precise, every twelve hours and thirty minutes, water from the southern coast of the Atlantic Ocean surges through the rocky portals of the bay. This immense amount of water is estimated to equal the twenty-four-hour flow of all rivers in the world combined.

Along the eastern bay, you can witness Fundy tides, the highest in the world, created by the bay's shape and dimension. Tides have been measured at 16 meters (52.5 feet)—the height of a fourteen-story-high building. As the water moves through the funnel-shaped bay, the bottom becomes more shallow, and the water literally "piles up" and is forced upshore. The length of the bay adds to the height of the tide because, as the low tide leaves, it collides with the newer, incoming tide. At Alma, the tide creeps quietly in, rising as much as a foot in seven minutes and often to a height of thirteen meters (forty-three feet) in six hours and thirteen minutes. Here, it is possible to walk on the ocean floor when the tide is out.

The Bay of Fundy's tides have caused many geographical changes in the area, battering the cliffs of Grand Manan, and creating the echo caves at St. Martins. The world's second largest whirlpool, Old Sow, off Deer Island, is also a formation of the tides. Twice daily the tides violently force the rapids of the Saint John River to flow upstream.

The tides have an immense impact on the daily life of its

The tremendous tides in the Bay of Fundy make New Brunswick's flowerpot rocks a popular tourist attraction. (Courtesy New Brunswick Department of Tourism)

inhabitants. Tides determine the times for shipping, fishing, and also influence the weather. Herring fishing is completely dependent on the currents of the tides. The water's motion provides food for local wildlife and is an important feeding stop for migrating birds. Some birds double their weight here, fueling themselves for their long journey to such places as the Arctic and South America.

One of the most popular attractions in eastern Canada are the flowerpot rocks at Hopewell Cape, where thousands of visitors travel to view the rise and fall of the Fundy tides. Another favorite place to explore the coast is along Route 114. Scenic Route 114 breaks off from the Trans-Canada Highway, so you can travel directly to the flowerpot rocks. This delightful journey is a breathtaking alternative to the heavily traveled Trans-Canada Highway.

The Floating Islands

On a calm, sunny day, the Manitou Islands sit peacefully in the North Bay, looking like any other islands in any lake. In 1615, Samuel de Champlain, the great cartographer, described the Great Manitou Island as "A very pleasant island, more than six leagues long, with three or four fine ponds and a number of fine meadows, bordered by woods that contain an abundance of game, which frequent the little ponds, where the Indians catch fish." But these heavily wooded islands are not like any others. Once a place of spiritual importance to the Nipissing Indians, the Manitou Islands are now said to be haunted and cursed.

The beginning of the curse goes back centuries. One legend tells of an Indian maiden named Snowbird who lived on the Manitou Islands. This Nipissing squaw ran away with an Iroquois brave because her tribe forbade them to marry. A small group of Nipissings pursued the pair and caught them. They dragged the couple back to the islands, burned the brave at the stake and forced Snowbird to watch. She struggled free and leapt into the flames to join her lover. The locals say you can still hear the cries of the dying maiden when you camp on the islands at night.

Another popular explanation for the curse is the story of a Nipissing tribe who lived on the Great Manitou Island. The group had fled there to escape an Iroquois attack sometime around 1650. In time, all the islands' wild game and fish were gone. Winter came and famine set in. The Nipissing tribe needed a sorceror to help them, so they chose an eleven-year-old girl for the role and sent her outside the camp to fast and prepare.

On the final day of her fast, a large sturgeon was suddenly found in a small pond on the island. With great joy, the entire tribe feasted to their hearts' content. But, when the girl returned to her father's hut the following day, she found snakes everywhere. The young girl saw that her father's lower body had turned into a huge snake. He told her, "Go leave this place. Go to our people at the Sturgeon River and tell them what you have seen here. This island is cursed. No one will ever be able to live here."

After hearing the girl's story, the tribe sent a small party to explore what had happened. All they found were deep, slimy tracks wedged in the snow leading to the pond.

More recent events have led the locals to believe that the curse really exists. There have been several tragic boating accidents around the islands and, to this day, no one has lived permanently on the great island. The beautiful long sandy beaches seem an ideal location for property development and summer cottages, but no such development has ever been successfully completed. There is ideal fishing on the island, yet no one vacations here. There were several attempts to mine uranium and thorium here in the 1950s, but these efforts were abandoned after the mine shafts mysteriously filled with water and bunkhouses burned down.

When there is fog and overcast skies, the islands seem to float above the horizon and eerie sounds seem to echo across the water from their hidden caverns. Many believe that the islands "float" because they are haunted.

Ice Hockey

You cannot truly appreciate Canada without accepting that hockey is more than just the national sport. The passion of millions, ice hockey is comparable only to the combined popularity of professional football and baseball in the United States. Hockey demands toughness, strength, and incredible endurance: players scramble on ice, sometimes brutally, for a tiny black puck that moves too quickly for the human eye to follow. Children as young as five years old begin to learn the game and play competitively; tickets for Stanley Cup Championship games are nearly impossible to find; and rivalries such as the one between Montreal and Quebec City can be quite violent.

Ice hockey's roots began in Europe, where field hockey was a popular sport. In the mid-nineteenth century, a large number of British troops were posted to duty in Canada and found the long, cold winters boring. Many soldiers brought along ice skates and field hockey sticks. Making the best of the cold icy weather, the soldiers began playing a form of field hockey, on ice. Further troops were sent to remote outposts in western Canada and the new game quickly spread across the country.

At first, there were no precise rules for the new "ice hockey." Rules were made up as players went along, depending on the number of skaters available, the condition of the ice, and the size of the playing field. Many cities across Canada from Halifax to Montreal lay claim to where the formal version of hockey was born. Most historians tend to agree, however, that Kingston, Ontario is the site of the first organized ice hockey game. In 1867, soldiers belonging to the Royal Canadian Rifles stationed in Kingston shoveled snow off a local frozen harbor and played hockey. Kingston thus became known as the birthplace of ice hockey, and the first hockey hall of fame was established there. In 1885, the first official hockey league in North America began in Kingston and was comprised of four teams: the Athletics, the Kingstons, Royal Military College, and Queens University. Queens University became the first champion of the league, defeating the Athletics with a 3–1 victory.

Many changes have occurred since. In the early days, the players' skates were exceptionally crude; everyday boots or shoes were worn with "spring" skates attached to the bottoms. Ambitious Canadian entrepreneurs, realizing the financial potential of the new sport, soon developed covered ice rinks. Sometime during the last two decades of the nineteenth century, the ball was replaced by a flat puck, and the playing area was reduced. In the early days, the teams consisted of nine players (a total of sixteen skaters at a time on the ice with two tending goal). This was reduced to seven-man teams when one of a pair of teams scheduled to play at the 1886 Montreal Winter Carnival showed up with two players missing, and the opposing team agreed to drop two players to form seven-man squads. Players found that they enjoyed the game more with less men on the ice, and soon the smaller teams became the rule.

Students at McGill University in Montreal played an eighteen-man game in March, 1875. According to historians, it was at this game that the sport was called "ice hockey" for the first time. Historians believe it was also at McGill that the first set of official game rules were set; many of them adapted from existing rugby, lacrosse, field hockey, and polo regulations. Ironically, one early rule forbade the use of bodychecking!

The Canadians enjoy long winters and natural ice is avail-

The Stanley Cup is ice hockey's most coveted prize. (Courtesy The Hockey Hall of Fame)

able from as early as October through March. By the 1880s, a Montreal company began manufacturing ice-hockey sticks and hockey was blossoming throughout the country.

Lord Stanley, governor-general of Canada, was very fond of ice hockey. He built an outdoor rink for his two sons, Algie and Arthur, who were devoted to the sport. The boys organized a team with local guards from a military unit and named their squad the Rideau Rebels. The Rebels played around the world and challenged the famous Ottawa City Club for the Canadian championship in the late 1890s. At this time, a victorious team had little to show for their win, so Lord Stanley commissioned a British silversmith in 1892 to create a special trophy: a silver bowl with a gold-finished interior. The first Stanley Cup was won in 1893 by the Montreal Athletic Association, who hadn't even engaged in a single play-off game! The Ottawa Hockey Club demanded

The goalie for the Edmonton Oilers blocks a shot. (Courtesy
Edmonton Convention & Tourism Authority/photo
by Ray Giguere)

the cup because they believed they were the best team in
Canada. The trustees of the Ontario Hockey Association
ordered the Ottawa team to meet a challenger but the idea
was rejected by the Ottawa players. So the trustees treated
Ottawa as if they were suspended and scanned the records
of the just-completed season: Ottawa had lost to the Montreal Athletic Assocation. The Ontario Hockey Association
declared the Montreal Athletic Association the champions
of the season and immediately dispatched the cup to Montreal.

To date, the Montreal Canadians have won the Stanley
Cup more times than any other team, claiming 23 champi-
onships. Runner-up Toronto Maple Leafs has won less than
half this amount. The Stanley Cup is still the most sought
after, highest achievement a professional hockey team can

hope to win. Since the popularity of ice hockey has spread into the United States, the Canadians have sometimes had trouble retaining their championship title.

Founded in 1943, the Hockey Hall of Fame in Toronto, Ontario houses ice-hockey memorabilia including the famous Stanley Cup. A vast array of historical uniforms, equipment, photographs, video displays of big games, and trophies from around the world will delight ice-hockey enthusiasts.

A shrine to the history and study of ice hockey, one of the museum's most important functions is the selection of honored members from one of three categories: Builder (great contributors to the development of hockey), Player, and Referee. Great hockey figures are selected by a committee consisting of former players, reporters, and broadcasters, each well-versed in the history, tradition, and skills of the game. By the end of 1986, there were 256 honored members: sixty-eight builders, 179 players, and nine referees whose portraits are accompanied by a biographical sketch.

Located at the Exhibition Place on Lake Shore Boulevard, the Hockey Hall of Fame is close to downtown Toronto. During the summer (mid-May to mid-August) it is open Tuesday through Sunday from 10 A.M. to 7 P.M. and Mondays from 10 A.M. to 5 P.M. Hours vary during the late summer from mid-August to Labor Day. Winter hours (September to mid-May) the museum is open from 10 A.M. to 4:30 P.M. and is closed on Mondays. Call the museum at (416) 595–1345 to confirm hours, as it closes periodically when exhibits are expanded.

The Calgary Exhibition and Stampede

Far from Texas, closer to the North Pole, the world's top professional cowboys compete for the largest purse of rodeo prize money in the world. The great event is the ten-day long Calgary Exhibition and Stampede with over $500,000 in prize money.

In 1912 a cowboy named Guy Weadick, a member of a traveling "Wild West" show, envisioned Calgary as the cross-roads of the Canadian West. He thought it could be the location of the biggest "frontier days show the world has ever seen . . . hundreds of cowboys and cowgirls, thousands of Indians . . . we'll have Mexican ropers and riders . . . we'll make Buffalo Bill's Wild West Extravaganza look like a side show . . ." This cowboy was a showman, a performer, and a promoter and an organizer, but he needed investors. Soon the "Big Four" were assembled, all prominent Calgarians: George Lane, A. E. Cross, A. J. MacLean, and Patrick Burns, who agreed to back the project to a total of $100,000. The show would be known as the "Stampede" and if it proved successful, they would turn the Stampede into an annual world event.

The stage was set and ready for the "Greatest Outdoor Show on Earth." The first Stampede, held in September of 1912, was a hit—opening performances were attended by over 14,000 enthusiastic fans. Unfortunately, a number of unforeseen expenses prevented it from being a financial success, and the rodeo was put on the back burner while Weadick left Calgary to work on other shows.

In the spring of 1919, Weadick returned to Calgary and the original "Big Four" were once again interested in financing the operation, providing Weadick could find thirty other local investors to contribute $1,000 each. This was accomplished with little difficulty, and local citizens have continued their support every year since.

The Stampede incorporated the local Calgary Exhibition in the early 1920s. Weadick was elated and wanted to highlight a special feature at the event. He chose chuckwagon racing, an activity drawn from his own experience on range round ups when crews raced their chuckwagons to the nearest town after a long day on the range. The last crew to arrive in town had to treat the winners to a round of drinks. This experience gave birth to the Rangeland Derby.

In 1923, the Calgary Exhibition and Stampede became a winning combination of great rodeo excitement and a celebration of the agricultural industry of Southern Alberta. The first official chuckwagon races in history were held and His Royal Highness, the Prince of Wales presented the silver trophy to the Canadian Bronc Riding Champion.

Since its initiation, the Calgary Exhibition and Stampede has expanded from a traditional six-day-long event to ten days. Attendance rose by over 145,000. In 1982, the Stampede introduced the richest purse offered in the history of the rodeo, the Half Million Dollar Rodeo. Hundreds of cowboys compete in elimination rounds leading up to a final day of winner-take-all competition. Over $250,000 in prize money is given to the infield, with winners taking home $50,000 in each major event. Today, over twelve million people visit Calgary (population 650,000) to watch the Exhibition and Stampede.

Rodeo stock, bred for competition, is used in daring events such as saddlebroncing, bareback riding, calf roping,

Calgary Stampede's chuckwagon event. (Courtesy Calgary Exhibition and Stampede)

steer wrestling, and bull riding. The highlight of the Stampede is the chuckwagon event where four wagon teams, each pulled by four horses, race around a half-mile long course.

The livestock show features the International Blacksmith's Competition, championship auctioneers, a cutting horse competition, steer classic, and over a dozen purebred livestock shows. The horses come in all sizes, ranging from large and powerful ones to toy-sized miniature horses, less than thirty-four inches in height. Other features at the Stampede include an old frontier western town and an authentic Indian village representing the tribes found in the area.

The Calgary Exhibition and Stampede takes place each July, a beautiful time of the year to visit Calgary. Daytime temperatures are around 24 degrees C. (75 degrees F.) with sunshine virtually guaranteed. The home of the 1988 Winter Olympic Games is only a ninety-minute drive from the Rocky Mountains and Lake Louise. For more information on the Exhibition and Stampede, call (800) 661–1260 or (403) 261–0101.

Festivals of Quebec City

Throughout the year, Quebec City offers several festivals and cultural events that make each visit to the city a unique experience. Every season is filled with festivities, but the highlights of the year in Quebec are the famous Winter Carnival and the International Summer Festival.

In February, blanketed under winter snows, Quebec City is a real winter wonderland. The Winter Carnival (Carnival d'Hiver), dating back hundreds of years, is a ten-day carnival featuring a variety of events, from ice-sculpture competitions to parades both during the day and at night by torchlight, and a famous canoe ride through the ice of the Saint Lawrence River. Over one million visitors attend the world-known event annually and enjoy the snow-covered city in its fairytale-like setting.

Bonhomme, a snowman, is the festival's mascot. Bonhomme enters the city more than a month before the festival and is greeted by the mayor of Quebec and presented with the keys to the city. During the carnival, Bonhomme is the king of the festivities, warmly welcoming visitors to Quebec with a cold handshake.

Quebec City is less than thirty minutes from four major ski resorts, which are open from late-November to late-April; snowfall averages more than 3.5 meters (130 inches) and assures you a long ski season. Cross-country enthusiasts will enjoy skiing on the famed Plains of Abraham, a 235-acre park in the heart of town. A special skibus operates daily and transports skiers between the major hotels and ski centers.

A clown entertains the crowds at Quebec City's Summer Festival. (Courtesy Communaute Urbaine de Québec-OTCCUQ)

Bonhomme greets visitors at the Quebec Winter Carnival. (Courtesy Communaute Urbaine de Québec-OTCCUQ)

For help with making reservations at local hotels, motels, inns, auberges, and condominiums, call (800) 463–1568.

The annual International Summer Festival (Festival d'Eté) is held during July. Now recognized as the largest cultural event in the international French-speaking world, the festival is a celebration of the performing arts, including music, dance, mime, and theater and featuring leading artists from Africa, Asia, Europe, and America. The Festival d'Eté has over 250 shows and more than 600 performers. Visitors walk through the city's streets to watch the outdoor events, and there are also stages and seating set up all over the entire town. The *MV Louis Jolliet,* a pleasure boat that tours the Saint Lawrence River, offers performances onboard in a great setting allowing you to enjoy the entertainment and a scenic view of the historic city from the water.

For more information on festivals in Quebec, call the Quebec City Region Tourism and Convention Bureau at (418) 522–3511.

Winterlude

One of Ottawa's oldest traditions is the most spectacular winter festival in Canada. The first Winterlude festival took place in 1979 in a city-wide effort to bring back old wintertime traditions of the nineteenth century. When harsh winter weather forced nineteenth-century Ottawa to be closed off from the rest of the world, residents would gather for a series of celebrations aimed at passing the cold season in a setting of comradery and fun. Traditional festivities include nonstop rounds of sleigh parties, curling competitions, sing-alongs, amateur theatricals, toboggan runs, and ice skating to music on rinks throughout the city.

Winterlude is a ten-day-long event offering over 200 activities and amusements for the whole family. What began as a

Winterlude's barrel-jumping competition. (Courtesy Canada's Capitol Visitors and Convention Bureau)

small local festival, now draws international competitors, with participants from across the country and around the world.

Competitions such as the Molson Trotting Classic, where horses venture across the ice, is a crowd-drawing highlight at the festival, as is snowboarding, a combination of surfing, skiing, and skateboarding. Contestants travel thousands of miles to compete in the World Outdoor Barrel-Jumping Competition, the Long Distance Skating Championship, and the International Snow Sculpting Championship.

Widely known as the longest skating rink in the world is

Skating on the Rideau Canal in Ottawa. (Courtesy Canada's Capitol Visitors and Convention Bureau)

Sleighs glide past snow sculptures along the Rideau Canal. (Courtesy Canada's Capitol Visitors and Convention Bureau)

the Rideau Canal, a man-made channel, open to the public, that runs throughout the heart of the city. Originally built for military purposes between 1826 and 1832, the canal now offers recreational activities throughout the entire year. The canal is over five miles in length and runs right through Ottawa. During the winter, the canal is used by businessmen who skate to work and on a sunny winter weekend, it is crowded with thousands of bright-jacketed skaters. Hot chocolate stands and a restaurant operate along the banks of the canal to serve hungry skaters. If you don't own skates, there are several rental outlets along the Rideau Canal. You can also rent a sleigh for the baby.

During Winterlude, Ottawa becomes a village of snow sculptures. Ice-carving workshops are held for those who have no previous experience, where experts will teach you the art for free.

If the winter festivities put you in the mood to ski, there are ten superior ski resorts within fifteen minutes of the city. Ottawa lies along the steep southern edge of the Canadian Shield, offering good alpine skiing opportunities in the countryside. Services at the resorts include lessons, rental equipment, night skiing, and canteens. Camp Fortune (819) 827–1717, Edelweiss Valley (819) 459–2328, and Mount Pakenham (613) 564–0247 offer good ski areas. There is also fantastic cross-country skiing in the nearby Gatineau Park, which is less than fifteen minutes from the Parliament Hill. There are over 200 kilometers (180 miles) of ski trails for everyone from novices to experts. Maps of trails are available at the Capital Visitors' Center at 14 Metcalfe Street (opposite Parliament Hill) and equipment may be rented at Camp Fortune.

Winterlude's official mascots are the Ice Hog family, made up of Mr. and Mrs. Ice Hog and their children, Nuomi and Nuoma. You will see them at any of the official Winterlude sites.

It's not difficult to get around Ottawa during the festivities. All five official Winterlude sites are linked by a regular shuttle service. For assistance with planning your trip and securing accommodations in Canada's capital, just call the Visitors' Center at (613) 239–5000 or (800) 267–7285 (in Canada from Central Ontario eastwards to Nova Scotia); or (800) 267–0450 (from other parts of Canada and the continental United States).

Festival of Spring

Springtime is a beautiful season in Ottawa—parks are awash with millions of tulips and the city is carpeted with color.

The Festival of Spring in Ottawa is usually held for nine days in the middle of May, as millions of tulips and other floral displays burst into color throughout the city. Highlights of the festival include hundreds of brightly colored tulip beds, a boat flotilla on the Rideau Canal, outdoor concerts and movies, a giant craft market, and fireworks.

Millions of colorful tulips are sent annually to the people of Ottawa from the Netherlands government in gratitude for the refuge granted the Dutch royal family during World War II. During the war, the Netherlands were occupied by German troops, and the royal family fled to Canada. Princess Juliana was pregnant at the time, and expected to deliver shortly. The only problem was that if she gave birth on foreign soil, her child could not be an heir to the throne. The Ottawan officials came up with a solution: they proclaimed a small portion of the city as Dutch territory, and the expectant mother would give birth there. The solution worked, and the tiny heiress was born a Dutch citizen.

Ottawa and The Hague were officially twinned in 1984 as a sign of the continuing bond between these two countries.

Unique Festivals, Only in Manitoba

On any given weekend, you can plan your time around a wide selection of festivals throughout Manitoba in northern Canada. Typically, they are celebrations with ethnic themes, but many are sheer silliness! Communities gather to race frogs, pigs, chickens, turtles, and, of course, there is always a dog-sledding competition.

Frog-jumping contests started in St. Pierre-Jolys in 1970 when the people of this small French-speaking town wanted something unusual to highlight their annual fair. The Frog Follies was born, and large, oversized frogs were suddenly in demand for reasons other than for their meaty legs. The frog-jumping contest is the main event: The frogs must cover the greatest distance possible in three hops, encouraged by a trainer pounding the platform from the rear. Trophies are awarded for the longest overall hop, the best jump in the finals, and the highest number of good jumps.

In Otterburne, there is even a more unusual celebration. Here, pigs are the heroes of the day. The Pig Rodeo (Rodéo du Couchon) began in 1978 when a local hog owner came up with the idea and offered to supply the contestants. Pigs are difficult to convince to run in the right direction, so this rodeo will provide a good chuckle. Another event, the pig scramble, pits teams of two people against a pig, which must be caught and tethered with a rubber band.

Visitors to the Boissevain Turtle Derby are greeted by 35-foot Tommy the Turtle. (Courtesy Travel Manitoba)

The Chicken Derby of Oakbank, just northeast of Winnipeg, is held in early summer each year. If you do not have a chicken on hand, you can rent one to enter in one of many events. It is more difficult to race a chicken than it sounds, but worth the price to see them parade by decked out in hysterical costumes.

The Boissevain Turtle Derby is in southwest Manitoba, only sixteen miles north of the United States border. The festival's mascot is an eleven-meter- (thirty-five-foot-) high statue named "Tommy the Turtle." Turtles are placed in cages behind the world's only electric turtle-starting gate and they race around a twenty-four-foot (seven-meter) course. The Turtle Derby attracts experienced contestants from across Canada and the United States. A final heat pits the Canadian and American champions for the world-turtle title.

Where would you expect to find snowmobiles racing at top speeds during the middle of a hot July? The Manitoba Swamp Skimming Championship separates the sinkers from the skimmers. This bizarre event requires drivers to cross the 475-foot width of the swamp; successful participants then attempt to cross the 1400-foot length. Speed is the most important factor, so with this in mind, many contestants remove extra weight on their machines, including their windshields and seats. Some snowmobiles reach speeds up to seventy-three mph (117 km/hr). The biggest hazard at the Swamp Skimming Championship is the recovery of submerged machines from depths of up to fourteen feet (four meters). Rescues are made by a Swamp Ranger and crew.

These festivals of the North Lands provide an experience unique to Canada. Here, turtles, pigs, chickens, frogs, and swamp skimmers have the chance to attain stardom, much to the delight of audiences worldwide.

La Paz Trappers' Festival

The La Paz Trappers' Festival, an authentic celebration of northern Canadian life, takes place during subzero weather each February in the Manitoba town of La Paz, 700 kilometers (435 miles) north of Winnipeg. The Trappers' Festival celebrates the lives of the tough and skillful trappers who have come to symbolize the heartiness of northern Canadians.

The World Championship Dog Race at the Trappers' Festival.
(Courtesy Travel Manitoba)

La Paz Trappers' Festival tree-swing competition.
(Courtesy Travel Manitoba)

The skills on which trappers relied while living in the harsh weather conditions are the basis for the contests held at the Trappers' Festival, including tree climbing, starting wood fires, tree felling and wood splitting, carrying 1,000 pounds of flour, muskrat skinning, moose calling, and running thirteen kilometers (8 miles) on snowshoes.

The main event at this festival is the World Championship Dog Race, first held in 1916 by a group of old-time trappers, prospectors, and fur traders. The dog-sled race is run in three 56-kilometers (35-mile) laps on the frozen, snow-covered Saskatchewan River over three successive days. Competitors travel from all over North America to race for a purse totaling over $35,000.

Other highlights of the festival include ice sculpture contests, professional and local entertainers, a fur fashion show, and, of course, the crowning of the Fur Queen. Food is also a major attraction, as visitors travel miles just to taste authentic native food such as fresh sturgeon, smoked fish, and moose stew. Also popular is bannock, once the staple of the trapline, a mouth-watering, shortbread-like treat.

Over 6,000 people travel from such faraway places as Europe and Japan to the small community of La Paz each year for the festival, more than doubling the town's population. For more information, contact the Northern Manitoba Trappers' Festival at (204) 623–3459 or (204) 623–3824.